MENSWEAR

20 Timeless Elements of Style

WHITE STAR PUBLISHERS

Edited by
VALERIA MANFERTO DE FABIANIS

Text by
GIUSEPPE CECCARELLI

Editorial assistant
GIORGIA RAINERI

Graphic design
MARIA CUCCHI

CONTENTS

2-3 A symbol of prosperity since the early 1900s, the white shirt is still an essential clothing item of the male wardrobe, as in the case of this one by Turnbull & Asser.

5 One of the critical points of the jacket is the neckline and the way it hugs the neck at the sides and back. A well-made jacket does not "detach itself from the neck" even during movement, but rather wraps itself around the shirt collar without creating any awkward gaps.

INTRODUCTION

Dressing is a serious matter. Especially for a man. Much has changed since the early nineteenth century, when man became an actor in what is called "the great renunciation" by assuming the role of male escort to a woman, thereby depriving himself of a certain degree of creativity and sophistication in favor of a kind of black-and-white uniform. Nevertheless, this aesthetic reductiveness never meant simplicity. On the contrary, the syntax of the male wardrobe grew increasingly complex, especially in the years when the concept of dress was bound exclusively to a formalwear so tightly structured that even simple items like a white T-shirt could cause a veritable revolution in attire. As Catullus used to say, "I hate and I love," words that sum up the universal ambivalence of the double relationship created by the nearly irreconcilable opposition—as it occasionally appears—between man and the act of dressing. On the one hand, a strict and detailed code that expresses elegance, nobility, care, and commitment; on the other, a nearly one-dimensional approach bound to basic needs and the rejection of superfluous elements. Actually, if one looks closely, every moment in time is an expression of a search for identity and a key cultural narrative. For far too long among the aficionados of men's fashion, those looking back with nostalgia have been set in opposition to the avant-garde, with the former a bit suspicious and snobbish towards the latter. Dressing is a continuum, a manifestation of a state of being in the world, and men too try to express this through their clothing. As in the case of language, the observer's point of view must not be didactic, but descriptive. Clothing, like language, is a living organism that changes in response to reality. The rules of grammar and syntax must be known but treated as tools for understanding, rather than as precepts. In this volume we look at the evolution of male attire through the lens of twenty iconic clothing items, and how, in various ways, it presented men from the mid-nineteenth century to the present, as well as at the needs and cultural trajectories that transformed "simple" clothing items into iconic objects that transcend categories, functions, and periods. Each item has its own story and, like a word, follows an unexpected path. We try to trace precisely how each of them unfolded; in some cases, it was more important to relate their history, in others, how they are made or worn. We keep the range of interest broad and well rounded, and try to give each item a voice, yet at the same time full treatment and a tone that respects its nature. In this way, we work out a rich and varied narrative of a particular domain—the male wardrobe—that is neither short nor boring, as the sacred history of style would have us believe. Dressing is an extension not only of the individual but also—and to an even greater extent—of the cultural and social mindset. "Icon" means just that: gathering instances of a historical moment and rendering them universal. And in this respect, the male universe has much to tell in order to reclaim its role as the co-star that the history of fashion expects of it.

7 Like so many actors of his time, Cary Grant flaunts a formal suit interpreted in an ironic key during a photo shoot. His class has remained intact over time.

8-9 Initially formal and classic, men's fashion has evolved over the course of years, adapting to the needs of society without, however, losing its identity.

TAILORED SUIT

FORMAL EXCELLENCE

Ava Gardner often said, "I've never heard a man announce: 'I have to leave; there's another man wearing the same outfit.' Men don't worry if they're all dressed alike. It means that they haven't made any mistakes." We could practically state that male attire places homogeneity above variety. Indeed, since 1800, precise and irrevocable rules have defined the rules of the elegant man's wardrobe for every occasion. The precision and meticulousness of the cut have thus become decisive factors, and sartorial techniques have noticeably evolved, enabling the creation of garments that follow the contours of the body more closely and elegantly without impeding freedom of movement. For a man, speaking about clothing means having to treat the dearest thing in his closet with sensitivity. Following the dictates of such a long tradition is not only a means of avoiding errors, but also a way of sharing a code of rules. The stage on which this ritual takes place is definitely that of the tailor's shop, home of the slow but inexorable art of meticulous construction, stitch by stitch. A true gentleman has two options: *bespoke* or *made to measure*. The first refers to the production of an utterly original and one-of-a-kind garment; the second, on the other hand, consists of an adaptation of a mass-produced item—albeit of high quality—to the customer's measurements. Were we to write a short guide to proper attire, we would have to deal with three basic types of information: the cut, the occasion, and the type. The suit as a form of daily attire—jacket, trousers, and a vest cut from the same fabric—came into being in the 1930s.

11 A paragon of elegance and style, Clark Gable epitomizes the Golden Age of Hollywood between the 1930s and the 1950s.

Since the 1950s, the vest has steadily diminished in importance but has never fully disappeared from the male wardrobe. The first great tradition arose in England, on the so-called *golden mile* of Savile Row, the site of the British aristocracy's famous tailors: Anderson & Sheppard, J. Dege & Skinner, Huntsman, Henry Poole & Co, Davies & Son, Kilgour, Gieves & Hawkes.

12 The quality and consistency of English style can only be attained by adhering to the high standards set by London tailors Anderson & Sheppard, whose apprentices learn directly from the expert hands of their masters.

13 left Fabrics are the soul of every custom tailored men's suit—everything starts with them. The choice should be based on the type of garment desired, though men generally aim for style, elegance, and comfort when it comes to made-to-order items.

13 right Anderson & Sheppard suits stand out for their natural cut, which follows the body and facilitates movement, a feature that has been passed down for decades.

14–15 Work in a tailor shop is never-ending. At Henry Poole's, for example, tailors are committed to combining the most sacred traditions with a modern approach. Customers can choose from over 6,000 styles.

15 right Every suit made by Henry Poole is numbered and registered, so that the shop is able to retrieve and reconstruct any element if it requires repair, and the shape of the suit can be maintained and receive due care.

16 A Gieves & Hawkes pattern comes to life when the customer is called in for a first fitting, and when defects and the adjustments needed to customize the suit to his physique become apparent.

16-17 Know-how cannot always be properly communicated from one person to another, even when experts are involved. This is why every Gieves & Hawkes client is assigned a tailor, who over time gains sufficient experience to recognize his demands.

The twentieth century, however, witnessed the rise of the Neapolitan school and a philosophy of dress very different from that of the English—a trend that revealed that Italy, and not only Naples, had an equal say when it came to men's fashion. Tailors such as Cesare Attolini, Rubinacci, and more recently Kiton have turned Naples into a capital of menswear, as Caraceni did for Rome and Campagna for Milan. The time-honored tradition of maintaining a low profile runs counter to the utterly Italian attention paid to appearance; the social and class consciousness of "Those of us who wear Savile Row suits," as more conservative customers say, vanishes before the typically Neapolitan freedom of personal expression. The Englishman simply wants to dress in the correct manner; the Italian wishes to be elegant. Thus, in actual fact, choosing a suit means above all choosing a philosophy of life. In both cases, possession of a top-notch tailored suit requires a great deal of patience: a minimum of 7-8 weeks, and considerably more for a high quality bespoke. It is the occasion above all that dictates the choice of fabric and color. For office wear, it is better to steer towards fabrics defined as "drapery," namely, ones woven out of pure wool, or wool blended with synthetic or artificial fibers, and which, depending on the type of yarn and processing, are said to be "combed," "carded," or "fulled." Tweed and herringbone are best for leisurewear. These fall into the category of "carded."

18 Attolini, a company founded in Naples in 1930, revolutionized the way in which men's suits were crafted, effectively giving birth to the Neapolitan style, as in the case here.

The types confront us with a superficially simple choice: two-piece, three-piece or double-breasted? Reaching for the first or second is a mere matter of personal taste and social context. In some workplaces, high-standard formality is looked upon with favor, just as in others the vest seems obsolete. When it comes to double-breasted, on the other hand, we are immediately accosted with what is still a lively controversy. The double-breasted jacket has had its ups and downs; according to some, it helps slim down the silhouette and is thus flattering for everybody; according to others, however, it is good only for those with a well-proportioned, more or less slender silhouette. Bruce J. Boyer recently stepped in to resolve the matter, claiming that "no man, regardless of his shape, should be afraid to wear a tuxedo," to which he added a sound piece of advice: "If you like it, wear it!" Surely an illustrious case in point is that of "The Lawyer" Gianni Agnelli, who was portrayed innumerable times in a double-breasted jacket, an item that accompanied him throughout his life. One early photograph depicts him in his twenties in a beautiful light-colored, double-breasted Caraceni suit. No doubt thousands of subtle reasons lie behind the choice of any suit, but the sole true criterion is the quality of the cut, which must fit like a glove and show off the figure. A lower-quality fabric with a smart cut is always preferable than the reverse.

The key for judging the wearability of a suit lies in the shoulders, which must be broad enough to allow the outer edge of the sleeves to drop freely and straight down, but not so wide as to fatten the figure. The classic rule of thumb is that the sleeve be of just the right length to offer a glimpse of the shirt cuff—a few millimeters when the arm is hanging straight down, and a generous centimeter (half an inch or 1.3 cm, to be exact) when the elbow is flexed at the height of the stomach. The jacket must also be broad enough across the chest so that it can remain buttoned even when the person is seated. Among this code of rules, however, is a golden one that must always be followed: a respect for proportions. Elegance, as is known, is synonymous with equilibrium, and equilibrium is attained through a combination of details that make all the difference. In one of very few interviews in which he discussed the matter of style, Cary Grant observed: "In my job, I have collected dozens of different suits over the years, but they all have one thing in common: they're timeless. In other words, the neck is never too narrow or too wide, the pants never too long or too short." The male wardrobe is a microcosm of measures and proportions that goes beyond the mere production of items according to a millimetric scale that characterizes *prêt-à-porter*. Equally important in any choice of jacket is the "cran" (the angle of the neck to the jacket's lapels), which has an impact on proportion. A high cran in the Neapolitan style leads to a longer lapel, which makes the chest seem longer. Similarly, side vents cut above the pockets make the figure seem taller. By contrast, a low cran and shallow vents tend to compress the figure. When it comes to slacks, on the other hand, the width at the bottom of the leg depends on the person's height. According to the aforementioned rule of equilibrium, it should neither be so wide as to cover half the shoe, nor so narrow as to impede movement. Widths change with the use of pleats, especially double ones; in such case, the trousers must be seductively soft at the pelvis so that the pleats not spread open. The rule of fine taste prefers the single pleat for heavy fabrics or slack worn as separates, and reserves the double one for suits or lightweight fabrics. For a man, therefore, dressing is not as easy as it sounds. The alchemy that unites rules, occasions, and personality leads to a difficult process of negotiation.

21 Described as the "well dressed man," Cary Grant became an icon in spite of himself because he looked perfect in any role and any suit.

SHIRT

EFFORTLESS ELEGANCE

Language has been heavily influenced by the shirt, which we find in dozens of figures of speech. It stands as a symbol for a way of life; at the same time it is the sign and significance of a man's relationship with the world and other men. (The expression "to roll up one's sleeves," for example, betokens the station that a man can reach through commitment and willpower.) Over time, the shirt has been elevated to represent something that speaks of the most intimate and important part of any man: his ability or inability to assert his identity. All these meanings have not been lost over the course of time. Although they may seem obsolete today, they continue to affect us, consciously or not, whenever we choose a shirt or even more so when we custom order one. As already noted, tailoring is a personalized form of labor, which, thanks to its ritual nature, possesses a very special type of magic.

23 It's the symbol of style that transcends fashion. The archetype of elegance in its clean, pure color, neat lines and the grace of its collar, the white shirt is to the male wardrobe what the black sheath dress is to the female one. It's impossible not to have one.

Describing its world in a book, Silvia Venturini Fendi explains how "there is an affective value in the artisanal product, one that arises from the personal relationship between the person who creates it and the person who wears it, and is fostered by moments of intimacy and various emotions." And this is more true than ever when it comes to making a shirt. In the cobbled streets of Rome's historic center, Piero Albertelli has been making them since 1967 and would be able to recount the history of the leading figures of our century simply by organizing the information disclosed to him in confidence during fitting sessions for his shirts. "When one wears a shirt, there's something inside it, something that can be read in its weave, a human dimension, a confidence," whispers Albertelli. "Everyone from Kennedy to Valentino has passed through here, from De Niro, when he was in Rome shooting *Once Upon a Time in America*, to Gianni Agnelli. Making a shirt is an intimate act; it's necessary above all to be a psychologist, a confidant; 70% of our work depends on who we are as people." What presides over its design is thus a one-to-one, man-to-man relationship. The iconographic popularity of this garment is bound to a precise style: the white shirt that became the absolute archetype of menswear. The designer Massimo Piombo came up with an original and quite apt definition of it: "The white shirt is the very basis of fashion. It is the ultimate expression of the will and the knowledge needed to make an object that is genuinely pure. The white shirt is the equivalent of mental purity."

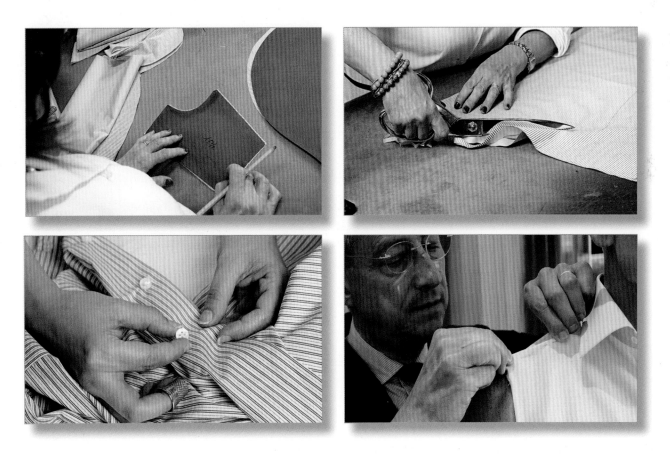

24 Albertelli is a one-of-a-kind shirtmaker because he still believes that one needs to inspire with love the garments that one makes. This sort of philosophy compels clients to return time and time again to his shop in Rome's historic center.

25 The most prestigious shirts are made entirely by hand. Albertelli and his tailors personally cut the fabric of each shirt, prepare the buttonholes, and sew the buttons and collar, all of which can be custom-made according to the client's measurements.

Crystal clear, essential, it is the mirror of a man and his soul. It is no coincidence that in the 1700s it was viewed as an undergarment and was slipped over the head, and that until the dawn of the twentieth century, white was a sign of wealth and could only be worn by those who, not having to work, did not risk impairing its whiteness. And if one wishes to recover the beauty of some of its antique flavor today, one needs to take certain details into consideration. First of all, the fabric. Cotton and linen are the most suitable and common materials for a top-quality men's shirt, given that silk—another fabric widely used in the past—is truly stuff for connoisseurs, of whom there are hardly any left today. Since they must be line-dried, silk shirts are sewn only for use in the summer. "Years ago," recalls Albertelli, "Gustavo Lombardo, founder of the movie production company Titanus, used to come to my place each summer and order silk shirts. Even then he was one of the few who knew that silk had to be line-dried." Thus except in the case of these rare items, if we want a casual shirt we should choose Oxford cloth, the fairly simple weave of which produces a soft but highly durable fabric; poplin or batiste, which have a more peculiar weave in that the threads of the weft are thicker than those of the warp, work better with a more formal and elegant style.

26 Gianni Agnelli—aka "The Lawyer"—was adamant about certain details of his attire; he knew exactly what he wanted or did not want to wear, and when, as, for example, this white shirt while vacationing at the seaside.

27 The harmony of all the parts that go into a shirt arises from the quality of the individual components, not least of which is the fabric, as in this example sewn by Giovanni Inglese for Agnelli.

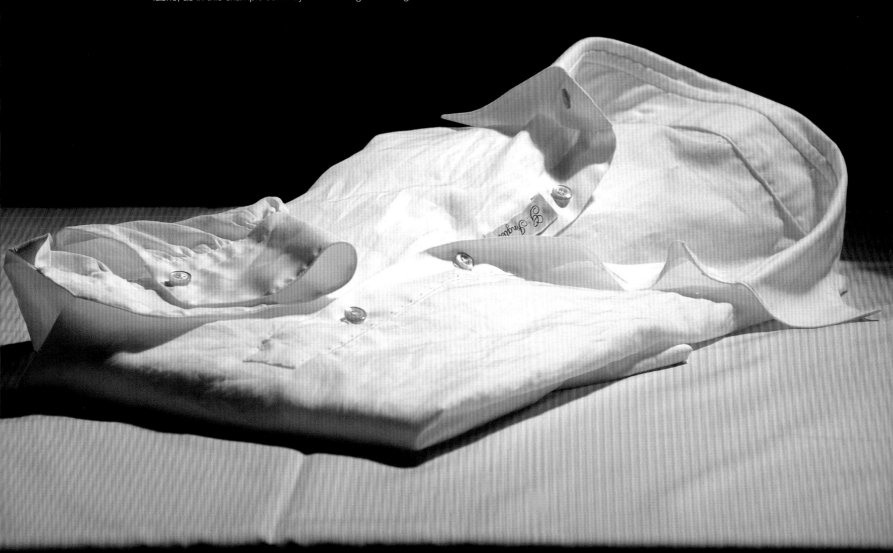

"I like to think that in today's dictionary of elegance, the white shirt is a universally used term. Which, however, everyone pronounces as he pleases."

(Gianfranco Ferré)

Wilbur's TRADE **DOUBLE WEAR** MARK

COLLARS FIT

Every quarter inch length in highest possible grade.

25¢

2½ inches high **Vogue FIVE FOLD**

EVERY STYLE MADE IN THREE GRADES

IF YOUR DEALER CANNOT SUPPLY YOU, WE WILL. 25¢ 20¢ *and 2 for* 25¢

WILBUR SHIRT & COLLAR CO. TROY, N.Y.

The collar is undoubtedly one of the most important details on a shirt. Initially there was only the Mandarin collar, but in the 1930s the so-called reversible collar took the upper hand and won the lead. Back then, both collars had one thing in common; they were detachable. In this way the collar could be washed separately and the rest of the shirt spared needless wear and tear. The most popular are the turndown and the Italian collar, which manage to be formal without being too flashy. The distance between the tips may vary and should be chosen according to the tie with which the shirt is paired. The height is calculated in the same way, on the basis of its own material quality. Spread, Windsor, and French collars are by far the most common. They can be worn with or without a tie; in the case of the first, more space is left for the knot, which thus attracts more attention to itself. It is advisable to wear fairly wide neckties and to tie medium-sized knots that fill up the entire space. The pin collar's tips are shorter than those of the turndown collar and are fastened by pins of various form. Beloved by Americans, it has never been fully embraced by Europeans.

30 The detachable stiff collar is believed to have been invented by Hannah Montague in Troy (upstate New York) in 1827, after she removed the collar from one of her husband's shirts in order to wash it, then reattached it by stitching it back on.

31 An example of a pin collar that requires a pin to fasten the knot of the type of tie that this collar demands. A wide knot is recommended.

Another very popular one is the soft roll or button-down collar, in which the tips are literally buttoned to the shirt. This is a style invented by Brooks Brothers, and one that purists to this day feel has been practically impossible for any other shirtmaker to duplicate. As for the other styles, essential landmarks for shirt buffs include Charvet in Paris, the English shirtmakers on Jermyn Street, Barba in Naples, and Truzzi in Milan. Finally, the cuff may have one or two buttons, and rounded or square ends, but most importantly, it must have an additional button with a hand-sewn horizontal eyelet on the sleeve placket along the forearm. Last but not least comes the embroidered monogram—the most prestigious detail— usually located on the left side, slightly above the waist, in print or cursive letters. Form and material are thus equally important in defining the shirt's iconic status. The details define the object, while the men who wear it, the symbol.

32 For a man an embroidered monogram on a shirt is a detail of unquestionable value. It should be located on the front, in a place where it will not be visible when the jacket is buttoned—usually on the left side, 4 cm (1.5 inch) above the waistline of the trousers.

33 Apart from some slight variations, white, light blue, and pink are the most classic colors for business shirts as they go easily with another great classic of the male wardrobe—the regimental tie.

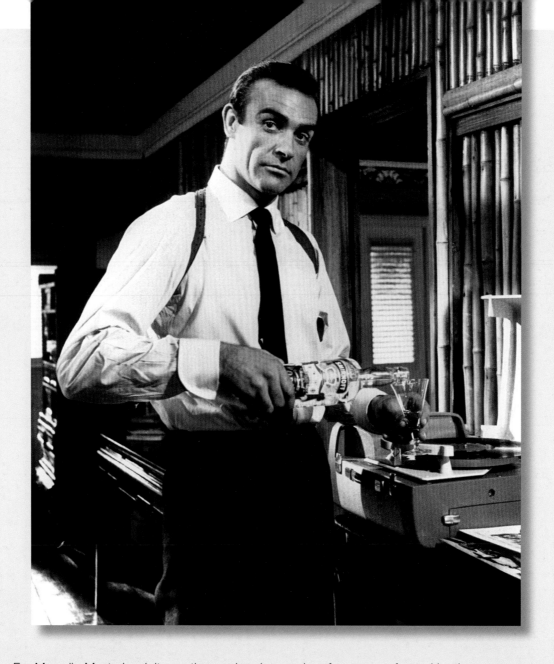

For Marcello Mastroianni, it was the nearly naive candor of a man confronted by the great mystery of life, as much when he wore it in a movie such as *8 1/2* as in his personal life. James Dean's short-lived career, on the other hand, left us with an image of social rebellion, of generational rage when, in *Giant*, he changed from a denim to a white shirt. Sensual and lecherous in his loose, half-open shirt in *American Gigolo*, Richard Gere epitomized the contemptuous careerism of the 1980s. Cultured, sophisticated, nearly impenetrable, was the white one belonging to David Lynch, for example, which he wore both on the red carpet and while painting in his studio. For John Travolta and Samuel L. Jackson in *Pulp Fiction*, it represented the rigor that needed to be observed in a world full of temptation, the nearly mystical law of the outlaw. In any case, it always speaks of a man's personal qualities, of an iconographic manifestation of a state of mind, of a mode of being in this world. For this reason, a shirt is never simply a shirt.

34 Male iconography as a fashion statement arose in the 1950s thanks to actors such as Sean Connery, who, dressed as Agent 007, always wore Turnbull & Asser white shirts.

35 The Italian actor Marcello Mastroianni used to wear a classic white shirt on both the movie set and in private life.

TIE

LOVE IT, HATE IT, WEAR IT

Yes or no to the necktie? That is the question. The quarrel over the tie sees at times a battlefield. In the last ten years, decrees and prohibitions have tried to undermine its importance and very existence. It was in 1988 that the Dutch Prince Claus von Amsberg signed "The Declaration of the Necktie" that summoned participants to a public ceremony in which they liberated themselves from the oppression of the tie and embarked on a new course through the "paradise of open shirt-collars."

The "no tie" alliance thus hinges not on social status but choice of lifestyle. Famous episodes from America to England have by now indicated this tendency. At the Soho Club in New York City as at Shoreditch House in London, clients are obliged not to wear a tie. Imagine the astonishment of Mr. Mansel Fletcher, the famous English fashion and costume critic, when his tie was confiscated at the aforementioned club in East London. It made no difference that he was there to meet Michael Drake, the CEO of one of the world's key tie manufacturers. Wearing a tie speaks first and foremost of the act itself. Businessmen, politicians, and actors all have their preferences, which, like a session with a shrink, reveal their true personalities.

37 Michael Aldridge tying the knot of David Hemmings' tie. The two actors collaborated on the musical *Jeeves* in 1975.

Donald Trump embodies the perfect businessman, always dressed in a suit with a meticulous double-knotted tie in a glistening, brightly colored but generally tone-on-tone silk. In this instance, therefore, it conveys a strong, aggressive character who loves to demonstrate his power. Barak Obama always wears a blue or red tie paired with a dark suit. The first color is that of his party, the second, a symbol of power. Years ago, John F. Kennedy wore dark ties with a fine diamond pattern to project an image of modernity, reform-minded politics, while in 1984, Ronald Reagan wore Hugh Parsons ties, preferably those with the Regimental stripe—the classic necktie—due to their "conservative" connotations. Alternatively, there are actors like Robert Downey Jr., who always wear a thin, dark tie, as if referring to long periods in their lives, or conversely like Will Smith, who prefer the Windsor knot, a symbol of force and dynamism, like the characters they play on the big screen. Certainly these days no man can say, as did David Niven, "Tell me that I got my line but not my tie wrong."

All the same, those who choose to wear a tie must respect ironclad rules even today. Without delving too deep into its history, we can say that the tie as we know it was born in New York in 1924 thanks to Jesse Langsdorf, who cut fabric at a 45° bias angle to the selvage, using three strips of silk that he sewed together in succession. The idea was patented and exported all over the world. Even today, quality ties are still made following the same procedure. Silk is the principal material used, and the quality of a tie can be recognized by touch alone. Next comes the stitching. A good tie is usually comprised of three pieces of variously sized fabric that are sewn together. Careful examination will reveal that in higher quality ties the seams between individual parts are executed with a sewing machine. The stitches that give body to the tie on the inside, on the other hand, should be done by hand. There is no discourse on the tie that does not include a description of the knot. Until 1900, for what was then used as a tie, there was only one; in the 1930s, thanks to Edward, Prince of Wales, two more came into existence; in 1989, a fourth was discovered... yet, despite so many years of the tie's existence, only four ways of knotting were universally recognized. This provoked an act of defiance by two Cambridge physicists, who, wishing to liberate the fashion world from the inhibition of the knot, figured out all the physically possible ways to tie a knot based on a model of the movement of atoms, and came up with sensational total of 85. More specifically, however, if aesthetic criteria such as symmetry and equilibrium expressed in mathematical terms are taken into account, only 13 of these could be defined as elegant. The simple knot, the great classic of necktie knots, is by far the most widely used because it is fairly easy to make and works well with most ties and practically every type of shirt collar. The double knot looks thicker than the simple knot does, works well with most shirts, and is perfect with all ties except very thick ones. The little knot, in turn, works particularly well with thick ties, or shirts with narrow collars, but should be avoided with long or open collars. Although relatively easy to make, it involves making an 180-degree "twist." The Windsor knot is the one for special occasions. Very English, its name derives from the Duke of Windsor, who made it popular. In view of its voluminousness, it should be used with open—e.g. Italian or Windsor— collars. Sometimes difficult to tie, it must—to be perfect—fall at the exact center of the collar and hide the uppermost button of the shirt. Next we have the half Windsor, which resembles the Windsor but at the same time is less thick and easier to make. It goes perfectly with skinny or less thick ties. Elegant and triangular, it is preferably worn with a shirt that has either a classic or open collar. Finally, there's the four-in-hand, which can be paired with all ties, collars, and looks. The four-in-hand always assumes a slightly elongated shape, with the width at the middle of the tie determining the result.

38 Despite the many ways in which a man can make an impeccable knot in his tie, six standard steps ensure that he will never make a mistake. The Windsor or half Windsor knot is always the best choice.

English manufacturers stick the most closely to all of these rules. The most important among them are Drake's, Charles Hill, and Holliday & Brown. These supply ties to Gieves & Hawkes, Turnbull & Asser, Hilditch & Key. Among hand-made English ties, those at Tobias Tailors on Savile Row are of excellent quality. They are produced neither in a factory nor a manufacturing plant, but instead are sewn by an independent tie maker. This ensures that clients come to possess a one-of-a-kind item.

The best hand-sewn French ties are those made by Charvet. The shop on Place Vendôme—a masterpiece in the art of textiles—offers the largest selection in the world. Except, of course, for Hermès at 24 Faubourg St.-Honoré, which offers its fans one of the few models of the Seven Fold Tie, one cut from a single piece of silk and containing no seams—a standard feature of nearly all Neapolitan ties.

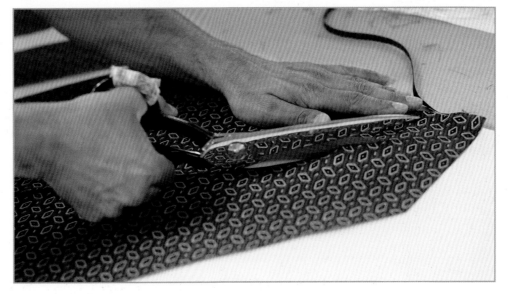

42 If fashion is not always paired with luxury and elegance, Hermès has managed to make one of the most controversial accessories for today's man by reinventing classic combinations with irony and fun.

43 Maison Hermès ties, a symbol of luxury par excellence, are known as the 7 tie due to the reduction of their width to 7 cm (2.7 inch). A way of updating a classic male wardrobe item while retaining the patterns that have brought fame to the French label.

As with the suit, so here the world that follows menswear is split between London and Naples. Two different types of ties traditionally produced by Neapolitan houses can be distinguished on the basis of the way in which the silk is worked—the tie in printed silk and the tie in woven silk. In the former, the pattern arises from juxtaposition, that is, the individual design motifs are printed in succession on the silk fabric. In the woven silk tie, on the other hand, the design is woven into the mesh of the fabric and is based on the way in which the threads of the warp and weft are combined. These are the sort found at Marinella, the indisputable king of Neapolitan tie makers, or Marzullo or Cilento, two of the other old houses. By now Marinella has become a veritable empire throughout the world thanks to the label's various styles. There is probably not a single man of power, or even a mere tie aficionado, who does not own a Marinella; it appears on everyone from Luchino Visconti to Vittorio De Sica, and from Aristotle Onassis and Albert of Monaco, all the way down to Prince Charles of England, through whom it poses a threat to the native land of elegant male attire. A business as large and a name as recognizable as Marinella's has provided its own ties with a microchip attesting to and copyrighting their authenticity, taking a step towards modernizing a timeless bastion of male attire. As did Hermès in order not to lose a public ever more attracted to technology by creating eight ties in a heavy twill and reducing the normal width from 9 to 8 cm (3.5 to 3 inch), or by introducing styles in totally new patterns with motifs such as USB sticks, binary codes, or on/off buttons. Technology collaborates with tradition and the Parisian house has invented—perhaps for its more lazy patrons—the Hermès Tie Break, an app full of useful tips.

44 Family business. Maurizio Marinella belongs to the third generation involved in the tie business. Since 1914—for over a one hundred years by now—this Neapolitan firm has been increasing its presence on the international market in leaps and bounds.

45 Micropatterns are a must for the ties of Neapolitan tailors as well; muted colors were especially dear to Don Eugenio, Marinella's founder, who when speaking of elegance always said, "Never a midnight-blue shirt or a bold red tie."

CUFFLINKS

THE DETAIL THAT MAKES STYLE

Putting together one's outfit means moving within a grid of rules, unwritten laws, personal awareness, and a vision shared by a community. The ability to harmonize these elements is the same as that belonging to a composer who writes a melody. Notes and chords converge to create a musical structure in exactly the same way as articles of dress come together to compose an outfit. The composer's imagination—like the style of one who loves to dress well—steers these elements towards the right combination. But if a melody is outstanding only when it contains some so-called "notes extraneous to harmony," then apparel too requires subtle forethought, tiny accessories that like chromatic *appoggiatura* highlight the look and underscore its merit and beauty. In the male wardrobe this role is played by cufflinks. Any assessment of cufflinks comes with an invariable axiom—they are the decisive note of the suit, without which its overall effect risks being spoiled. We are therefore dealing with tiny, highly precious objects, both in terms of the role that they play and the material of which they are fabricated. Along with the wristwatch, they are the man's true jewels; as often happens, the smaller ones are costlier and can reach sums as mind-boggling as the $4.2 million estimated price for a model created by Jacobs & Co., which passed into history as the most expensive of all time.

46 Until the late 1700s, cufflinks were known as "sleeve buttons." Although their origins are uncertain, the modern concept of cufflinks arose in the post-Renaissance period; before that, brooches or laces were used as closures.

49 top Canary Diamonds—that's the name of the most expensive cufflinks ever created by the Swiss firm Jacobs & Co. Octagonal in shape, they were made out of 18-karat white gold, and 21-karat canary-yellow diamonds combined with faceted 10.76-karat rectangular diamonds.

If we go further back into the history of cufflinks, the few bits of information about them are not random. One of these relates the beginnings of their success to Dumas' famous tale of *The Count of Monte Cristo*, his first novel, in which he describes the wonder and astonishing quality of the wee precious objects worn by the Baron Danglars. Within a short time, cufflinks became a distinctive feature of every modern gentleman. Nonetheless, it is their precious quality, especially in the case of antiques, that makes them one of the most coveted items by aficionados and collectors. Among the rules that demand compliance—a tradition dating back to the Middle Ages—is one stipulating that they be received only as gifts and never purchased for oneself. Towards the end of the Napoleonic era, Fabergé perfected his glazing technique and began exporting his objects worldwide. Following tradition, the Czarina of Russia gave a pair of Fabergé diamond and sapphire cufflinks to Nicholas Allen, the scion of the Harrogate family, for his Confirmation in 1910. These cufflinks, which have a fairly long history and are believed to date at least to 1894, are now among the most frequently cited by collectors around the world. Actually the origins of cufflinks are far more ancient. Purportedly they were already used in ancient Egypt, but their real success came only after 1500, when a genuine passion for these tiny objects—equally fueled by Louis XIV's obsession with jewels—developed in France and England in the course of the habitual disputes over style between these two perennially rival countries. Thus, though England claimed paternity rights over the accessory, it was in France that the term "wrist jewel" was first (in 1788) used. Tailors and jewelers thus began indulging themselves by fabricating them in all sorts of shapes and different materials, including gold, gemstones, and glass paste, which appeared on the scene in the early 1700s. Susan Jonas and Marilyn Nissenson, authors of one of the few monographs on the subject, tell of the myriad shapes they accidentally came across in the course of their research: from hunting horns to dogs, from anchors to fish and every type of animal, to guns, compasses, high-heeled shoes, and some even made out of human hair.

48 Since 1600 the English aristocracy and upper class has regarded cufflinks as an essential wardrobe accessory. The director Sir Richard Attenborough collected only the priciest ones.

49 botton The technique that goes into creating a "Cameo" is a genuine, hand-crafted art known since 400 BC. Cameos are carved from shells with great skill, and always depict Greco-Roman subjects or woman profiles.

50 top More than anyone else, His Majesty Prince Charles, the Prince of Wales, bears perfect witness to the value and symbolism embodied by cufflinks. As in this pair, in which the crown and his initials are combined.

50 bottom William and Kate are the new British royal couple and in this capacity take ambassadorial voyages around the world. On their first trip to Canada, they were honored by the Northwest Territories with a gift of a pair of platinum and gold cufflinks depicting polar bears.

51 top One example of Paul Flato's creative flair: gilded screws and bolts make for a truly original pair of cufflinks. He was considered the foremost jeweler of American celebrities, especially between the 1920s and the 1940s.

51 bottom Tareq Salahi, during a rally, wearing cufflinks with an image of the inauguration of the U.S. president in 2001.

Although the function of cufflinks sets limits on the size of the actual object, which has to pass through two eyelets, the inventive powers of their jewelers have not been compromised. Instead they have proven to be practically infinite, as can be seen from an anecdote about the designer Paul Flato, who in the 1930s created a pair out of nuts and bolts when he found himself without his beloved accessories just as he was about to depart for a gala. His invention was so well received that the orchestra conductor, Eddie Duchin, fell in love with it and had an exact replica made in gold.

The success of the cuff-link is hooked, as it's appropriate to say in this case, to the evolution of the shirt-cuff. Born of clear functional necessity, they had their ups and downs that followed the vicissitudes of fashion. The Victorian period, with its starched cuffs, gave cufflinks such a great boost that with the arrival of the Industrial Revolution and the invention of low-cost mass production, they were rampant even among Europe's petty bourgeoisie. It was the Duke of Windsor, who—it could be said unintentionally—later put a stop to their relentless dissemination. Although he advocated their use—if in no other way than by being a member of the aristocracy—he was also a fashion-addict (as we would say today), and his stylistic convictions rested predominantly on the principle of a sophisticated but simultaneously relaxed elegance and a preference for soft cuffs with plain buttons. Aside from this setback, it could be said that cufflinks have continued to be a piece of our century's social, fashion, and artisanal history. Their variety once again brings us back to musical technique; few things can create such an enormous and potentially infinite variety of patterns in the same way that seven notes can succeed in composing infinite harmonious melodies. The main styles can be counted on the fingers of one hand: the symmetrical one, the most elegant and difficult to wear due to its two equal ends being bound by a chain; the torpedo, the most common type, with its head attached to a capsule that can be slipped into the eyelet and made to clamp the cuff-link to the cuff. Next come the cuff-link with the bar, a simpler version of the symmetrical one, and more recently, the fabric type, shaped like a knot, which has grown quite popular. Their use and combination with various cuffs is increasingly left to the imagination and the style of the wearer, and for this reason references to the shops where these

small, high quality jewels can be purchased are far more interesting. Among the most important ones is Deakin & Francis, the official jeweler of the British royal family and the starting point for any aficionado. One might easily think that it offers only classic and extremely serious styles, but actually, as is customary among producers and cuff-link lovers, the shop carries plenty of ironic and playful ones as well. Even here it is possible to find original and surprising shapes. Asprey, the famous atelier that recently manufactured an $11,000 model designed by Angelina Jolie and Brad Pitt for a charitable cause, is likewise in London. Trianon, a New York boutique founded in 1979, offers styles that are as expensive as they are elegant. Equally original are the productions of another young British company, Alice Made This, which has succeeded in climbing to the top of the market in a short time. In Italy, and obviously in Naples, there is no shortage of shops that have contributed to the tradition of cufflinks; such is the case with the collection designed by Luca Rubinacci, scion of the family, who every year designs an exclusive limited collection of 100 pieces for his loyal customers. As Rubinacci himself tells us, "My father used to say that you should be visible without grabbing attention. I know the classic rules, I grew up among them, so I take the classic style and reinterpret it, whereas many others try to overdo it, getting it wrong." Whether rightly or wrongly, cufflinks make one visible, and, as suggested at the outset, are equivalent to those "extraneous notes" that can be used to match the character one wishes to bestow upon a melody in order to obtain the most beguiling result.

52 top Deakin & Francis has been creating some of the most expensive and original cufflinks in the world since 1786.

52 bottom left The Pitt-Jolie cobra created by Asprey in white gold, emeralds, and black diamonds.

52 bottom right Trianon cufflinks typically include precious and exotic materials, such as ebony and pearls, diamonds and mother-of-pearl, or aquamarine.

53 top Alice Made This, Bulgari, and Rubinacci create unique items in gold, diamonds, and mother-of-pearl.

53 bottom Cartier has been creating unconventional jewelry since 1847, and has become synonymous with luxury worldwide.

WATCH

MODERN TIMES

The psychology on which any successful choice of watch is based is definitely bound to the very depths of the male character. As Josh Sims tells us, the technical features of a watch are often far more sophisticated than those that a common—albeit expert—consumer might ever use, but this does not detract from the idea that the mere act of wearing "such a technically impressive object offers a man an incomparable virile thrill." It is no coincidence that watches have to do with two domains that bear great prestige for men: sports and the military. If Donald Norman is correct and every object possesses its own "accordance," that is, every thing speaks of its own function, suggesting the use for which it was intended in a game shared by its designer and user, then for a man the watch is an alter ego on which to project a need for technical performance. The chronograph, especially, is a symbol of precision, reliability, and stamina—traits associated with the male universe. From an altitude of 10,000 meters to a depth of 10,000 meters, the high-level performance of a "watch object" sets the limits—or rather, the lack of limits—of a man's sphere of action. The first wristwatch was actually created for women by Patek Philippe in the late nineteenth century; its use by men is credited to Louis Cartier, who in 1904 designed a model for his friend Alberto Santos-Dumont, a pioneering aviator who wished to have one to wear when flying.

55 Although in the early 20th century the wristwatch had already been known for decades, it was not yet particularly popular. The Cartier Santos-Dumont was the first model to impose itself on the male wardrobe.

56 left Alberto Santos-Dumont made aviation history for his brilliant 14-bis, the first fully motorized airplane, by which he rose from the ground and flew 60 meters in the Bois de Boulogne, Paris, on October 23, 1906.

56 right Cartier seems to have drawn inspiration for the design of the watch that he dedicated to Santos-Dumont from his friend's votive medal, which depicted St. Benedict of Nursia, the patron saint of Brazilian slaves.

Henceforth, the milestones in this sector—such as the IWC Mark XI, the Holy Grail of the watchmaker's world—were all inspired by or dedicated to pilots and the world of aeronautics. A basic—nearly martial—design, this model, launched in 1936, was inspired by the Junkers Ju 52, one of the most important types used by the German fleet. The technical innovation of the anti-magnetic system that was introduced in the IWC made it legendary. Actually, Vacheron Constantin and Tissot had already introduced this feature in their watches in 1915 and 1929, respectively, but no one before IWC had fine-tuned it as flawlessly to meet the needs of pilots.

57 top and bottom The Junkers Ju 52 marked a key moment in early aviation history. Dedicated to this aircraft, the IWC Mark XI model gave rise to a new passion: the watch as accessory. When the Mark XII entered the market in 1994, it made its predecessor one of the most sought after collector's items in the world.

The legendary Hour Angle appeared in more or less the same years, and was created by Longines following the precise instructions of Charles Lindbergh, who, after crossing the Atlantic, realized how the hour angle could be calculated and asked for a special winding button so that he could operate it while wearing gloves. In 1934, on the other hand, Gaston Breitling perfected the chronograph that he had invented in 1915 based on the need to calculate the correlation between the end of a flight and what remained of the fuel, as could be done with the Aerospace and Navitimer models.

58-59 and 59 bottom The Hour Angle dedicated to Lindbergh was just the first of Longines' many tributes to pilots, especially those who were pioneers in aviation, from 1931 on.

59 top Charles Lindbergh, known as "Lucky," probably never had any clear ideas about aviation until he crossed the Atlantic after devising a new way of flying thanks to the help of Longines.

But the history of such models is much longer; it would be unfair to this prestige sector if we did not mention the Longines Swissair model of 1943, or the concurrent Benrus Sky Chief, the Zenith Pilot, the Rolex Air King, or the Omega Speedmaster. In recent decades, the various watch manufacturers have been heavily investing in technological research that promises to significantly improve water resistance at great depths, counter pressure, and, of course, enhance waterproofing.

60 Longines Swissair models are dedicated to the pilots of the Swiss fleet of the 1950s.

61 top Breitling has been the leader in technical watches since 1884. Its stopwatches are so reliable that the company has become the official supplier of the Swiss Air Force. Its history is one of great prestige, especially considering that it is one of the last companies to remain independent.

61 bottom The history of the Omega Speedmaster dates back to 1957, when it was introduced as a stopwatch for races, completing the clock collection already in use by the official timekeeper of the Olympic Games. The first Speedmaster, known as the "Broad Arrow," was designed by Claude Baillod.

Though Rolex intuited the watch's tie to sports as early as 1926, when it used Mercedes Gleitze's swim across the English Channel to market its Oyster, the research boom of the early twentieth century owed much to the need for watches that—for military purposes—could operate underwater. This was the case with the Italian firm Guido Panerai and the Swiss firm Blancpain, which in the 1950s, at the request of the French army, designed Fifty Fathoms, a watch with special features for a special military unit known as the Nageurs de Combat. The involvement of a legendary diver such as Jacques Cousteau definitely marked a turning point in the field. Improvements in the techniques of scuba diving and its spread as a sport and amateur pastime opened up a new market to professional watchmakers. After collaborating with professional divers, Rolex launched its Submarine in 1953, followed by the Sea Dweller 2000 in the early 1960s.

62 Hans Wilsdorf founded Rolex in London in 1908 though World War I later forced the company to move to Switzerland. The name was invented by the entrepreneur himself because its pronunciation was identical in every language. The Rolex Oyster epitomizes much of the company's history.

63 top With the 1927 Oyster, Rolex came the first water- and dust-proof watch—whence arose the name "oyster," alluding to its protective, airtight seal, as in the case of the sea shell.

63 bottom The Sea-Dweller is a watch used at great depths. It was developed for COMEX and is provided not only with thicker glass to enhance resistance, but also a helium valve. Since 2008, the Deepsea model series has been coming up with watches with incredibly high depth coefficients.

Ever more sophisticated research on performance pushed technology beyond imagination allowing watches to make history in three models capable of incredible feats: the IWC Ocean 2000 in 1980, which could work at a depth of 2000 meters (6,560 ft); the Breitling Avenger Seawolf, which could work up to 3000 meters (9,840 ft), and finally the incredible Bell & Ross 1997 Hydro Challenger, which in the Mariana Trench worked at a depth of 11,000 meters (7 mi). Given all its feats, it is not surprising that the watch has now become a symbol of the strength, performance, and resistance that typify the stronger sex.

64 top The case of the Avenger Seawolf has a diameter of 44 mm and its patented crown is enclosed in an imposing crown-protector. The model is fitted with a decompression valve that enables it to balance out the difference in pressure between the interior and exterior.

64 bottom The most important technical innovation of the new IWC Aquatimer model lies in its external-internal rotating bezel.

65 Hydro Challenger entered the market in 1997; to inexpert eyes it might look like a banal quartz watch, but its technical performance at great depths is actually the best on record, thanks to the presence of mineral oils in its case.

The watch is tied to man's concept of himself and his masculinity—a status symbol whose role has been nurtured by key personalities who have worn various models. In the 1971 film *Le Mans*, for example, Steve McQueen wore the TAG Heuer Monaco which thereafter bore the name TAG Heuer Steve McQueen in his honor. The various agents 007 have brought fame to two key models, the first being the Rolex NATO Strap Submariner often worn by Sean Connery the second, a special edition of the Omega Seamaster Diver 300M, associated with the more recent 007, Daniel Craig. In the performance that won him an Oscar for his role in *Wall Street*, Michael Douglas wore an IWC Da Vinci Perpetual Calendar Edition Kurt Klaus on his wrist. Among the best performing watches, on the other hand, has been Vin Diesel's Jaeger-LeCoultre Deep Sea Chronograph in *Fast and Furious*. High speed, extreme luxury, power, and performance are the qualities demanded of a watch today.

66 In 1969, TAG Heuer came up with the Monaco, inspired by and dedicated to the Monaco Grand Prix and later worn by Steve McQueen in the 1971 movie *Le Mans*. Due to its sporadic success, the Monaco watch was put back on the market in 1988 and thoroughly updated in 2003, in the wake of the actor's revival.

IN CINEMAS OCTOBER 31

QUANTUM OF
SOLACE
007

JAMES BOND'S CHOICE.

Ω
OMEGA

67 left and bottom right It was the Oscar-winning costume designer Lindy Hemming who chose Omega as the watch for the 007 saga: "I said to myself that Commander Bond, navy officer, scuba diver, and discreet gentleman of the world, would have to wear the Seamaster with the blue dial."

67 top right The watch models and brands worn by actors have changed over the years and in the various chapters of the

Male competitiveness has no limits when it comes to watches; as in the case of artworks, models have reached exorbitant prices, from the Franck Muller Aeternitas Mega 4 valued at $2.7 million and the Louis Moinet Meteoris at $4.6 million, to the most expensive watch of all time, the Patek Philippe Henry Graves Supercomplication, which sold for $11 million. The watch has thus passed from being a practical accessory to a safe-haven asset, enumerated among items that acquire value over time and are thus worthwhile long-term investments. Indeed, between technological prowess and delirious bids, the quality that makes a watch a high-profile object, namely its manufacture, has remained intact. This is a feature that obviously excludes the entire new digital industry, which for the most part is snubbed by true connoisseurs of the genre. In his 1978 book, *The Hitchhikers Guide to the Galaxy*, writer Douglas Adams described a humanity so "primitive as to still believe that digital watches are a good idea."

68 The most complicated watch in the world. That could be the definition of the Franck Muller Aeternitas Mega 4, which can live up to every possible challenge. This piece is a marvel of technology thanks to its 1483 parts and 36 complications, of which 25 are visible.

69 Louis Moinet has designed an incredibly expensive collection. The peculiarity of the Meteoris series is that its four models contain some of the oldest fragments of meteorites ever to land on Earth. In addition to the diamonds framing its case, the Mars contains a fragment of the Jiddat al Harasis 479, a meteorite that fell to the Earth 180 million years ago.

70 The world of watches loves records. The Patek Philippe Henry Graves Supercomplication owes its origins to a competition between the automobile manufacturer James Ward Packard and the banker Henry Graves, who shelled out over 6,000 Swiss francs at the time simply to secure his name on the watch.

This pretty much sums up the position of those purists who are deeply attracted to all of a watch's "complexities." In slang the term "complexities" refers to all the indications and functions that go beyond the mere display of time, including complete calendars, perpetual calendars (i.e. those that indicate the day, the exact number of days in each month and year, including leap year), lunar phases indicating evening hours, and stopwatch functions. All these are designed with the help of technology but executed by expert hands that labor over every single gear and all the finishes invisible to the naked or inexperienced eye. Craftsmanship is still the most appreciated and sought after aspect of every respectable watch and one that no technology has yet been capable of undermining.

To open a watchcase is thus to open a door into a world in which every technical element is full of both history and labor and stands as a symbol of ancestral forces that grant substance to the idea that man represents strength and power. To conclude, one can go back to the words of Vitaniello Bonito, who, without exaggerating, claimed that "the watch was coupled with the image of the world, the metaphor of the body, the state, and celestial harmony."

SUSPENDERS

LET'S KEEP UP

The history of fashion has taught us that often things do not happen as they should, but rather live their own lives, and follow an unexpected but efficient course. This is the case with suspenders—an accessory to which no one would have assigned much importance and which were actually conceived with the precise function of being hidden. But instead, as in a Georges Méliès movie, these things took on a life of their own and tried to rewrite their seemingly sealed fate. During the French Revolution, the Huguenots would use a leather or fabric strip to hold up their trousers by running it from the front to the back of the waist. It was from this simple function that history's first dandy, Sir George Bryan, known as Beau Brummell, came up with the idea to improve the way trousers fit. It was he, in fact, who imported them and, in a sense, imposed them on England and on the male wardrobe. In 1822, in his shop on Pantan Street (Hay market), Albert Thurston made slight modifications to create the suspenders that we know today: two parallel strips running down the front, and in an X- or Y-shape down the back, fastened with clips, buckles, or buttons. The story could have ended here, but the adoption of this accessory by elegant British businessmen gave birth to a little ceremony that projected this practical invention into a new and unexpected dimension. Etiquette immediately intervened to define their use and impose some fixed rules.

72 Gary Cooper in 1931 wearing a pair of suspenders on the set of one of his movies. Use of the accessory was quite widespread in America in the 1930s, contrary to the situation in Europe.

The most important and strictest of these
was that they not be left in view, but be worn beneath a waistcoat or a tight-
ly buttoned jacket. This golden and irrefutable rule probably contributed to the success of the straps
over time. It may sound strange or even bizarre, but the heat wave that swept Europe in 1890 made its
mark—as often happens—on men's style. High temperatures forced them to lighten up their outfits by
eliminating the vest, and thereby restricting the use of suspenders, which, according to the rule, should
not be visible. No requiem was sung for the accessory in question, however. Although the taste for
suspenders was dwindling in Europe, it remained strong and solid in America; no man could get
dressed without donning a pair of suspenders to hold up the perfect line of his trousers. So much so
that in 1938 an attempt was made on Long Island to banish all those who wished to go without them.
The follies of an earlier age, we might say. Well, American loyalty towards suspenders is nearly legendary: respectable men have mythologized them since 1736, when Benjamin Franklin in-
structed that they be worn by the first volunteer fire brigade (to this day U.S. firefighters
wear red ones). Furthermore, between 1871 and 1894, several patents for
suspenders were granted in the U.S.—one of which was even named
after Mark Twain—under the heading "detachable and adjustable
shoulder strap for garments."

74 and 75 Suspenders from 1880. The use of X- or
Y-shaped suspenders attached to trousers with a clip,
buckle, or button was already widespread in this period.

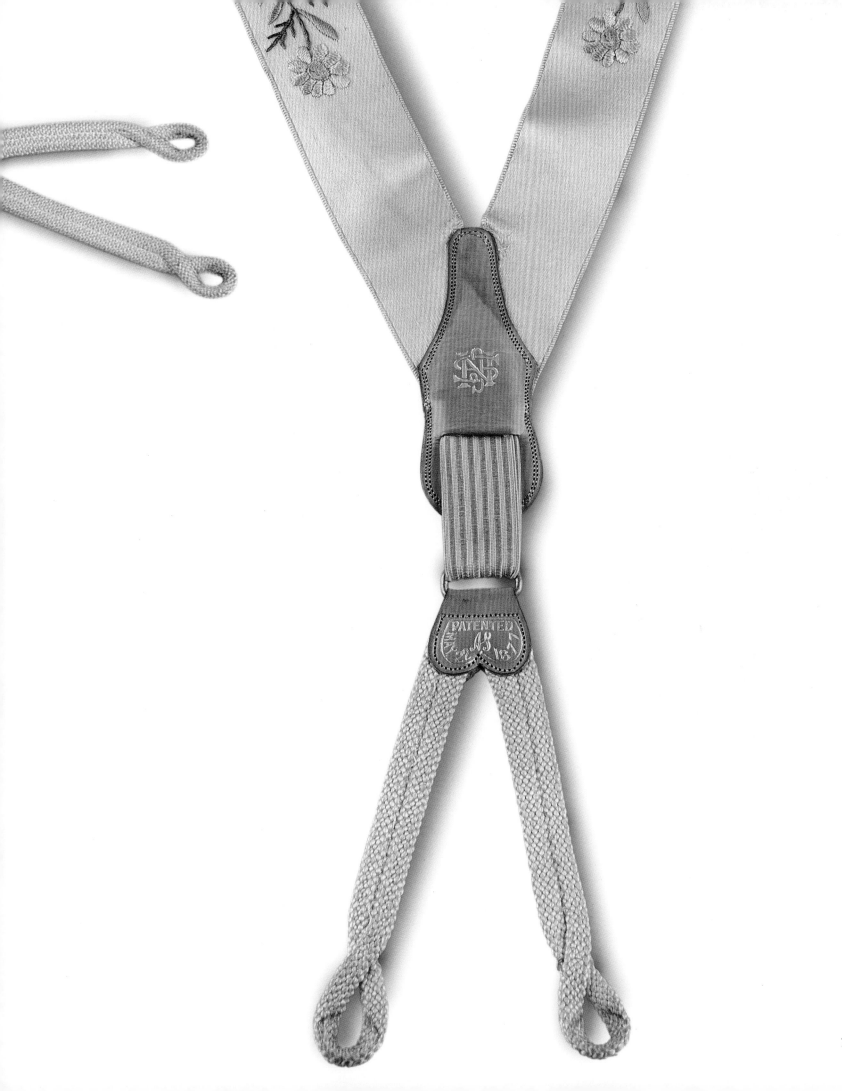

Americans were so attached to them that they broke every rule of etiquette to keep them in their wardrobe, using them indiscriminately with any type of attire and on any occasion. Every indicator that they were on their way to becoming a menswear staple was there: a useful and versatile accessory adored not only by members of the aristocracy but also by cowboys.

Etiquette has been updated, but is nonetheless always present. When worn with formal attire, they must be silk and match the suit; in the case of a tuxedo, they must be purely white and moiré. If worn with casual dress, they can be of any color or pattern, and made of felt or, more specifically, boxcloth, or leather. Some suspenders have elastic strips, edged in leather or fabric, only on the back. The ones sewn of boxcloth are sportier and more casual, while the grosgrain version is more suitable for elegant attire. Once their manner of use became established, suspenders became a legitimate feature of male iconography. They survived the 1930s and 1940s, holding up throughout Fred Astaire's dance numbers; in the 1960s, Cary Grant wore them beneath his suits, while John Wayne and Paul Newman wore them in full view, the former with jeans, the latter with an undershirt.

76 Fred Astaire and Ginger Rogers in a scene from the 1949 movie *The Barkleys of Broadway*. Tuxedo trousers, which as a rule come with no belt loops, are held up by thin suspenders.

77 In a scene from the movie *Lady L*, Paul Newman wears a pair of suspenders while displaying his notoriously irreverent look.

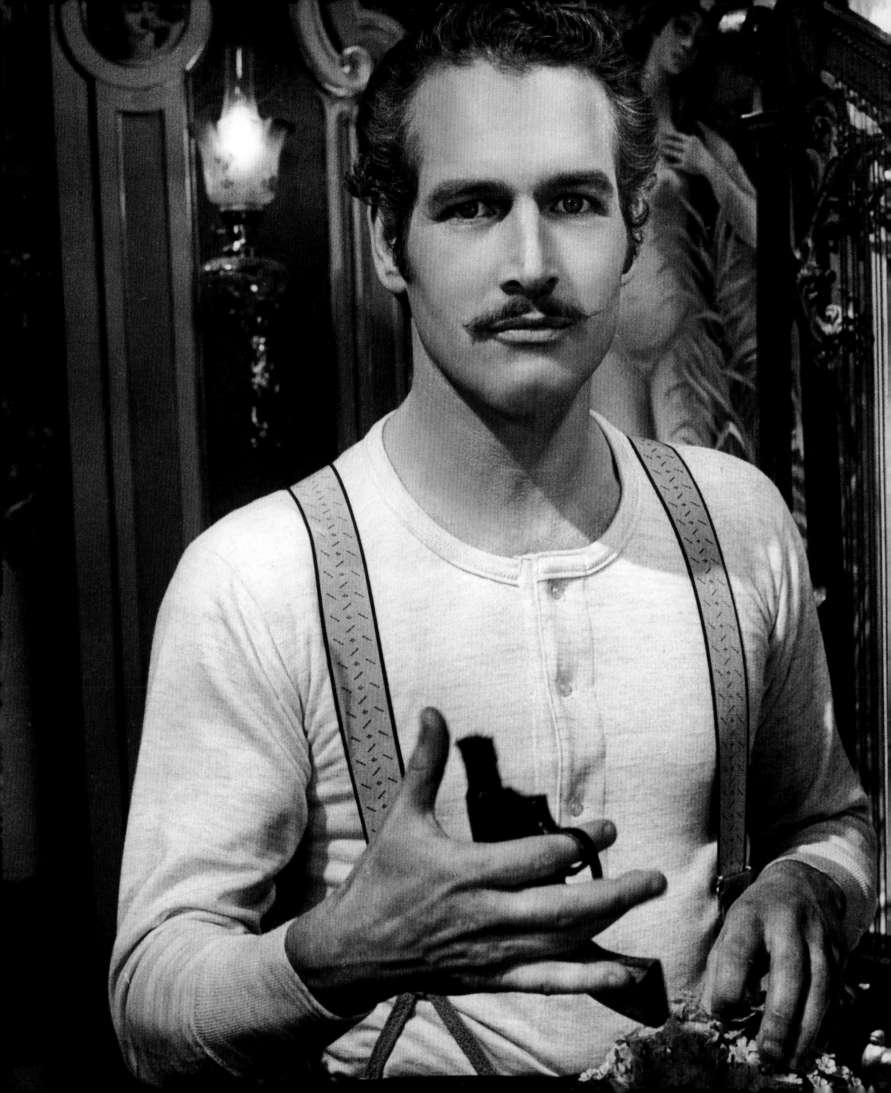

To the extent that, alternatively respected and desecrated—as legends are—they sometimes became an affectation, sometimes a symbol. This has happened in more recent times, when the most disparate characters have made a fine show of them. Such was the case with Johnny Depp, who turned them into an inevitable accessory of his alternative, nearly tribal look that combines the popular American traditions of cowboys and Indians, or of anchorman Larry King, who, in view of his profession as journalist, harks back to the iconography of the men's club to convey a sense of tradition and trustworthiness. Finally, there's author Jack Hirschman, who has turned them into a symbol of protest—a pair of red suspenders expressing his passion for politics and social commitment. Nowadays they are regarded mostly as an accessory for the connoisseur, even though any man who considers attire a means of personal expression continues to keep at least one pair in his closet. It is precisely for this reason that small "sanctuaries" with high-quality suspenders of the most varied shapes and styles still exist to this day. Worth a visit in the district of St. James in London, for example, are shops such as New & Lingwood, Harvie and Hudson and T.M. Lewin, marvelous places for those who are crazy about them. For those passing through Rome, there is no excuse for not visiting Cruciani & Bella in Piazza San Lorenzo in Lucina, or Sartoria Ripense on Via di Ripetta, a place that, albeit only recently, has recreated the world of classic male elegance of yesteryear in all its authenticity. And finally, "last but not least," one cannot omit Marinella in Naples, a mystical voyage into the magnificence of Neapolitan male elegance.

78 The American television journalist Larry King wearing a pair of his famous suspenders, which became his unmistakable trademark in his over 30-year long career on CNN.

79 Among young boys, wearing suspenders is a sign of affectation even today.

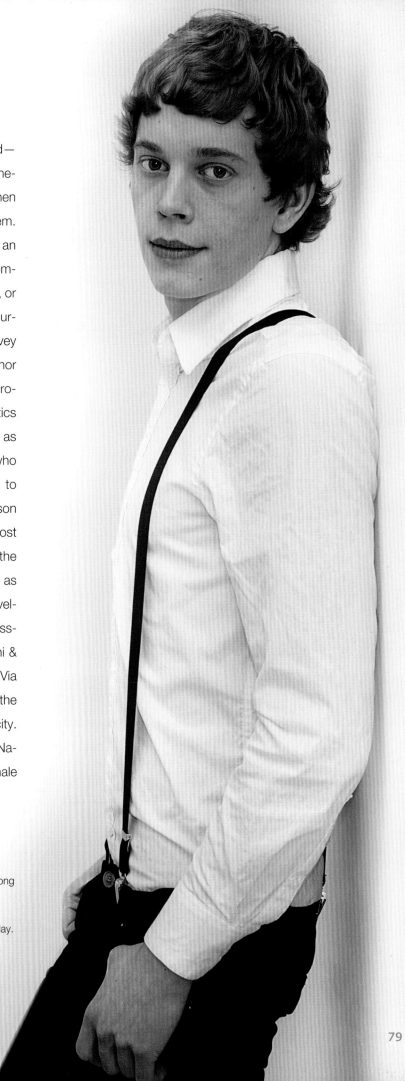

OXFORD

80 and 81 An Oxford model from Church's Crown collection created to celebrate the brand's historical merits and the tradition of high-end English shoemaking.

Carl Gustav Jung used the shoe metaphorically as a prescription for life and a psychological diagnosis, claiming that a shoe that fits one person may be too narrow to fit another. Without delving deeper into Jung's psychoanalytical implications, this statement does in fact offer us the necessary starting point from which to state that one feature of the classic shoe is its customization, especially with reference to the fit, even though the styles are rather well defined (as in the case of every item in the male wardrobe). Making an Oxford shoe is a complex process that is broken down into well-calibrated steps, but above all nearly ancestral actions. If over the years psychology has enjoyed investigating the hidden meaning of the fetish for women's shoes, then its approach to men has perhaps been more two dimensional but no less cogent, especially in the matter of the shoe's creation. Less aesthetics, more craftsmanship—this is the claim made by every shoemaker. A shoemaker's workshop is one of the most suggestive and evocative images in men's fashion—wooden molds piled up on shelves and paper patterns hanging from the ceiling. The ritual of a shoe's creation begins in fact with the measurement of the foot, one of the most intimate acts that a gentleman faces when putting together his wardrobe. As Carlo Marini—one of the oldest cobblers in Italy and one of the few who still makes everything by hand without using a machine for a single step—explains, "First thing is to take measurements. The client sits down

82 Workers intent on checking the quality of shoes made in a British shoe factory in 1936.
Anglo-Saxon shoemaking is famous for its high quality.

83 Cobblers busy joining various parts of the vamp to lining and tacking shoe parts onto molds in a factory in Northampton in 1949.

and has his feet measured: length, height, and instep. Then, the shape of the foot is traced on the pattern with him standing on the table. One needs to make sure that the pencil is held at a perfect 90° and that the tracing is as continuous as possible." And here starts the process of creating the unique, personal form of every shoe. Since 1899 Marini has been creating shoes in Rome for powerful and world famous men, and remains an eminent figure in the "art of shoemaking" in Italy and beyond. "Our clients include American oil tycoons and Saudi princes, but also celebrities like Robert De Niro or people like Gianni Agnelli or Sergio Leone." Once the measurements have been taken and the pattern created, a wooden mold is prepared; it is on this that the fine leather is modeled until it is perfectly molded over its

84 The historical molds are now exhibited as memorabilia. "The Lawyer" Gianni Agnelli, deemed one of the most elegant men of all time, was a steady client of the atelier Marini, as was Robert De Niro and many other great actors who often came to Rome during *la Dolce Vita*.

base. The first proof is produced from this prototype. If it is good, the shoe is made; otherwise it is necessary to start the process all over again. Unlike a garment, the wooden form cannot in fact be modified and it is necessary to remake it from scratch. To bring a pair of Oxfords into being thus requires a series of time-consuming gestures; though the time needed to do so varies significantly, it usually takes about two months. Marini is a family business with an archive of 6,000 patterns, the envy of every leading company in this sector. For it, as for the other great names in the shoe-making tradition both Italian and foreign, the steps and passion needed for the creation of high-quality shoes are the same. And it is precisely this process, so attentive to detail and history, that has made Oxford a unique icon in the male universe. The name presumably derived from the fact that in the 1820s students at the university of the same name revolted against the uncomfortable boots customarily forced on them, and began cutting them along the side. Soon the incisions moved towards the front, where the laces are fastened today, and the boot began its climb towards becoming the shoe known as the *Oxonian*. In 1846, Joseph Sparkes Hall, the shoemaker credited with inventing the Chelsea boot, declared to the *New Monthly Magazine* that the Oxonian was the most comfortable walking shoe thanks to its low cut and new system of lacing, and that it could be identified with Oxford. However, the same model was given different names in different countries: Balmoral in America, in reference to Balmoral Castle in Scotland, or Richelieu, in honor of the well-known cardinal, in France, whence the term Francesine can likewise be traced in Italy. Lace-up shoes can thus be divided into two great families: Oxfords and their closest variant known as the Derby, which has open laces and for this reason is deemed more casual, but in fact has an easier fit. As for everything else, they differ in terms of decoration and mode of production. There are two main techniques for creating an elegant and practically indestructible shoe: Blake and Goodyear.

85 top A portrait of Carlo Marini, who has been carrying on the family tradition since 1965 and transformed the Roman shop into an international brand.

85 bottom Some of the 6,000 molds belonging to the Marini archive. In the more than century of its existence, Marini has made shoes for some of the most famous men in the world, from politicians, to actors, to businessmen.

86 Classic models of brogue workmanship and perfect examples of the "country shoe." Tricker's top-selling style to this day.

87 Some Edward Green models waiting to undergo the final stages of assembly and the finishing process.

The Blake-Rapida method, one of the oldest, lies in joining the upper shoe to the sole by a double row of stitches, one on the inside (named after Blake) and one on the outside (the so-called Rapida), which make the shoe more solid and elegant, versatile and lightweight. The first of these attaches the lining of the insole and the upper shoe to the first sole; the second, which is done directly on the mold, joins everything to the second sole. The Goodyear technique derives from the first with the addition of a welt. This manufacturing process was patented by Charles Goodyear in 1839: the welt, a soft piece of leather glued along the perimeter of the shoe, is sewn to the leather rim of the insole, thus joining the upper shoe to the lining. The sole is sewn at a second stage. A padded middle sole, generally made of cork, is placed in the hollow between the insole and the sole, with the result being an elegant shoe, excellent and comfortable at the same time. Last come the decorations. Initially men's shoes were not provided with any sort of ornamentation, only much later did cobblers began decorating the upper shoe with tiny perforations. The punchwork on the tip, the so-called flowers, or grilled or ridged borders, are elements that gave rise to the full-brogue and the semi-brogue, according to the extent of the decoration. Brogue derives from the Celtic *brog*, which means shoe, and it is the very practice of punching shoes (popular among Scottish and Welsh peasants and laborers in order to release the water that seeps in during fieldwork) from which the name of this kind of workmanship derives. The "cobbling" tradition originated in England in the artisanal district of Northampton, only one hour's train ride from London, the site of all the great firms that produce "bench-made" shoes, that is ones crafted on the benches of master cobblers. Situated on Oliver Street, in a splendid and intact Victorian structure, John Lobb's company and shop are synonymous with elegant and custom-made shoes par excellence. At 56-60 Michael's Road, on the other hand, lies Tricker's, a unique firm that remains entirely in the founder family's hands under the direction of Nicholas Balthrop (fifth generation of shoe entrepreneurs). Tricker's is the opposite extreme—the country classic, elegant but solid and indestructible shoes, capable of lasting a lifetime. Then there's Edward Green at 74-76 Cowper Street, an institution like no other, the lord's shoe par excellence, a line in which every style assumes the name of a Prime Minister in recent British history and is characterized by the various forms of its shoes' soles. Equally classic and timeless is Crockett & Jones on Perry Street.

88-89 top   Inside Church's London flagship store, one of the brand's most exclusive shops.

88-89 bottom   A classic example of a Church's Oxford with its typical brogue workmanship, also known as "wingtip." The punchwork in this case is referred to as "full-brogue," whereas if it's limited to the tip without the lateral wings, it is known as "semi-brogue."

But there's one brand above all the rest that has become synonymous with men's shoes—Church's, established in 1873 on Maple Street. In 1880, the firm moved to Duke Street where it has remained ever since. Church's success definitely owes much to the family's business sense, particularly that of William, who was not only the first to introduce the concept of right and left to shoes, but also knew how to combine the modern notion of manufacturing with the ancient art of cobbling. Between 1892 and 1907, Church began exporting his own product, which became a yearned-for object among prominent men, first in Europe, then in North America. With the rise of the so-called "Made in Italy," the *Bel Paese* became the shoes' new El Dorado, and today Italian shoes may have surpassed English ones in fame and success. Companies such as Salvatore Ferragamo, Fratelli Rossetti, Santoni, Moreschi, and Silvano Lattanzi are the new names of the same object of desire: the lace-up shoe. The manufacturing regions are spread throughout the country, but are all comparable in terms of artisanal capability and high-quality goods. Like so many top-notch shoemakers in Italy, Paolo Scafora of Naples has updated the manufacturing process by creating plastic molds, "but only because wood warps with time," and thus perhaps in this one case the old art has been modernized for good reason. Yet, apart from such tiny innovations, a genuine man's shoe is still crafted in one manner, as it always has been.

90 and 91 Two images from Church's new advertising campaign directed at a young audience with a renewed focus on the firm's core business: classic styles in the English tradition.

NORTHAMPTON, ENGLAND

Church's

English shoes

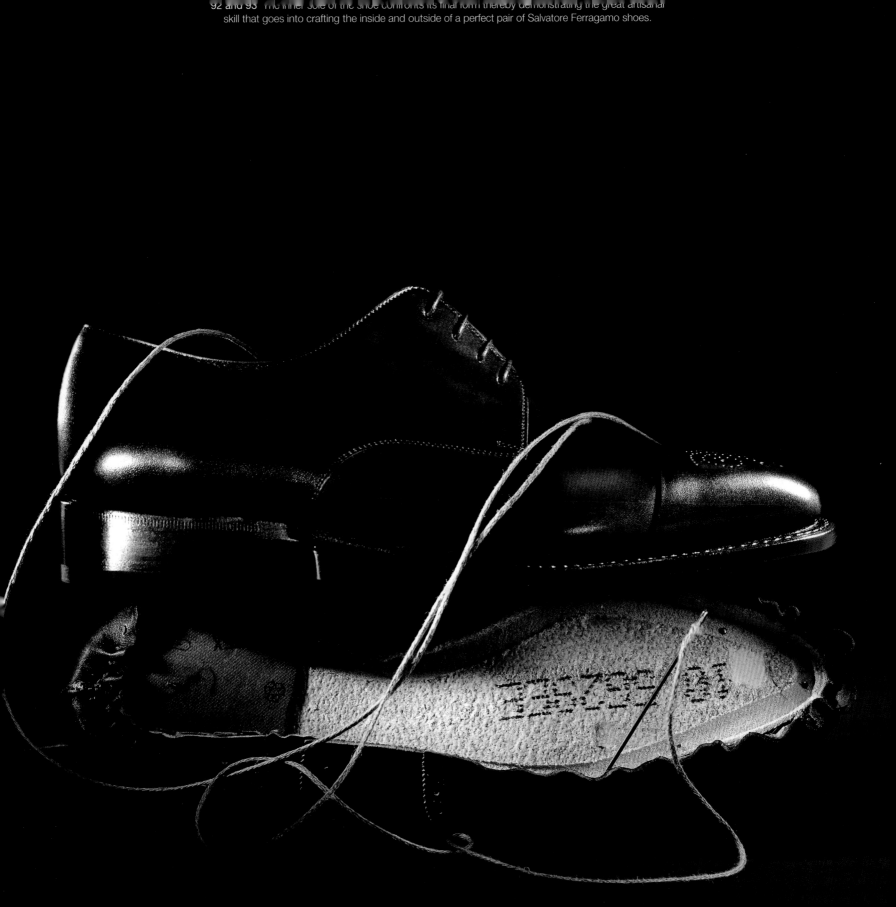

94 top The shank being hammered onto its mold in the Santoni laboratory to enhance a close fit and grant perfect form to the leather.

94 bottom Several stages of work on a shoe in Scafora's atelier. It is virtually an artist's studio, in which details define a prestigious universe, as relayed by the company's logo branded onto the sole.

95 Santoni's modern art of "cobbling" relies on plastic molds to avoid wood, which warps over time.

96 Bolts of leather, waiting to be cut in the Moreschi laboratory, are selected and organized according to color and "feel," the jargon used to describe the softness of the fabric.

97 A series of Moreschi vamps waiting to be attached to the sole, to which a heel has already been fixed. In industrial production quality control of various phases is likewise carried out by expert hands.

TRENCH

ADVENTURE COMPANION

The trench coat's reputation as one of the most universally worn garments is indebted above all to its enormous success on the big screen—a phenomenon bound to great movie classics such as the final scene in *Casablanca*, in which Humphrey Bogart, tightly wrapped in his Aquascutum trench coat, bids farewell to Ingrid Bergman. Or Robert Mitchum's worn-out look in *Out of the Past* (1947), where the coat enhances the mystery of the character's dark past. Or equally in Alain Delon's shady countenance in *The Samurai* (1967). Mystery is always a formidable lever that attracts and vanquishes. Beneath the allure is a downright deliberate act. So much so that at the beginning of the century, the eruptive and highly imaginative aesthetic force of the trench coat turned it into a fundamental style icon with such power of attraction that not even women could resist it. Mythical female stars of the golden age of cinema, such as Marlene Dietrich and Greta Garbo, who toyed with the ambiguities of androgyny, contributed much to the garment's fame. Yet at the same time the trench coat also worked in the reverse sense, reinforcing the indomitable femininity of Holly Golightly, alias Audrey Hepburn, in *Breakfast at Tiffany's*, or as a symbol of law in the case of countless unforgettable characters from the movies to television.

99 Before *Casablanca*, no one thought that it was possible to be cool during a downpour. Humphrey Bogart succeeded not only in being so, but also definitively altered the fate of the trench coat, which until that moment had been confined exclusively to the military establishment.

Peter Sellers demonstrates this in all the episodes of the *Pink Panther*, in which he strips the trench coat of the golden charm granted it by his predecessors to confer upon it the levity of timeless humor. Or it can assume the scruffiness of the seemingly absent-minded Inspector Colombo. The list of examples is so long that at a certain point one can no longer figure out what is responsible for its mythical status—the trench coat itself or Hollywood. A journey full of thrilling stopovers. 1982 was the year we first encountered a young Harrison Ford wearing one in *Blade Runner*, in which its resistance to water was put to a tough test by the constant downpour in the movie's various scenes. Rugged, ironic, feminine, androgynous, shrewd, disheveled, and melancholic, the trench coat can be all of these and much more. It has the capacity to transcend categories and decades, play disparate roles, and mock the passage of time. Warren Beatty can wear an acid-yellow, albeit timeless one in the blockbuster *Dick Tracy*, and Keanu Reeves a futuristic all-black one in *The Matrix*.

100 Unkempt in an eternally wrinkled trench coat—that was Inspector Colombo's look
in the television series of the same name.

101 Peter Sellers changed the image of the trench coat, endowing it with a semi-serious quality
in his 1976 movie, *The Pink Panther Strikes Again*.

The trench coat's native land is once again nineteenth-century England. In around 1870 two British fashion houses, Aquascutum and Burberry, registered two different waterproof, breathable fabrics, one of which was gabardine. The revolution sparked by these materials was immediately tapped by the Royal Army, which ordered "trench coats" first for the Crimean War, then for World War One. After the conflicts came to an end, the practicality, durability, and versatility of the trench coat made it a tremendous success in the civil sector. The two companies thus became giants in the clothing industry.

102 During World War I, Aquascutum created the first breathable rainproof trench coats for soldiers and officers.

103 Thanks to its versatility, the trench coat became an enormously successful item in both the military and civil sphere. The camel-colored, single-breasted Aquascutum Corby is one of the firm's most iconic styles.

Burberry was the one that became more closely identified with its item and that succeeded in building an empire around it. Originally, the trench coat was known as the Burberry Tielocken, which was patented by Thomas Burberry in 1912. This innovative model was secured by a belt and no buttons. Central to the history of the Burberry trench coat is the tightly woven fabric that distinguishes it from all others. Invented by Thomas Burberry in 1879, gabardine revolutionized rainwear. Every distinctive detail of the Burberry trench coat was introduced to meet a specific need. Burberry trench coats came to be manufactured in Castleford, a city in northern England, by expert craftsmen who combine traditional techniques with advanced modern technology. Each garment takes about three weeks to produce and requires over one hundred highly specialized procedures, each of which guarantees the quality and the unique look that has made the Burberry trench coat famous. One peculiarity in particular is the top-stitching along the neckline—180 tiny hand-sewn stitches on the collar—which gives it a soft curve that molds perfectly to the neck of the wearer. Another distinctive feature is "doubling over," a process by which two thin threads are intertwined to reinforce yarn. Next, strict control is maintained over the color of Burberry gabardine: drawing from the archive, one can choose from honey, stone, or black. Among the distinctive features that have become the British company's trademarks are the "checks" (in camel, ivory, red, and black) that characterize the coat's lining. These are sewn in mirror fashion on the inside and outside to ensure the pattern's continuity. The sole exception is the collar, on which the lining's unmistakable lines are angled at 45 degrees.

104 The success of the trench coat and its manufacturers, such as Burberry, was unprecedented in the volume of business generated. But even before its spread as a popular garment, Burberry made a significant marketing effort to promote what we now call the company's "core business"—the military trench coat.

105 The Burberry trench coat plays a chameleon-like role in contemporary culture. This item seems to express different semantics based on location or the person wearing it, but in every case it fits its context perfectly and generates new meaning.

> *"Fashion is a way of saying that you exist without having to speak."*
>
> (Rachel Zoe)

The trench coat has retained its original double-breasted shape for 150 years and is comprised of 26 pieces of gabardine, shoulder pads, a chin strap to prevent water seepage into the collar, a tartan lining, a short over-the-shoulder cape to shield against the cold, a triangular flap that covers the fastening on front and enables tighter closure, sleeves that can be pulled tight around the wrists with straps, a belt with brass eyelets, and a buttoned vent in the back. There are five styles that have remained fixed in time: the Heritage, which retains the traditional functional features designed for military use—such as the rear fold added to make the garment more comfortable on horseback—and which appears in various collections and lengths; the figure-hugging Sandringham, which comes in long and short; the Kensington, characterized by its modern, tailored cut and available in short and medium; the Wiltshire, likewise a modern cut of medium length with raglan sleeves; and the Westminster, the longest of the classic cuts. The inherently sartorial quality of the trench coat has certainly contributed to its reputation. It has turned the garment into a "nostalgic element [...] a fashion classic—writes Valerie Steele in *The Classy Rise of the Trench Coat.*—It is one of those objects that has become part of our everyday vocabulary." All this has rendered the coat iconic and even enabled designers to confront it over the years. From Armani to Versace, from Ralph Lauren to more avant-garde designers such as Comme des Garçons—all have taken on the trench coat. A veritable "trench coat fever" has continued for decades, infecting everyone from celebrities of the caliber of Justin Timberlake to ordinary folk, from politicians such as Winston Churchill to members of royal families, such as Prince Harry. Fate, however, has let it be violated without making it surrender. That's the power of a piece of iconic clothing. The final example is Pharrell Williams, who wears one in camouflage—an ideal tribute to the garment's origins.

107 Gabardine is a very old term that dates back to the Renaissance, and was used in France and Spain to indicate the work clothes of laborers. Its ruggedness has thus been noted since 1500. Its special weave grants it the perfect balance of strength and manageability, so much so that it is now used not only for trench coats.

FEDORA AND PANAMA

PRECISELY AT COCK

Talk about the "irony of fate"! In the history of fashion and costume it is not unusual for destiny to play wily tricks while debunking seemingly inherent and immutable axioms. One of the most powerful symbols of masculinity today, the Fedora, actually originated with a woman, the actress Sarah Bernhardt, who in 1882 played the role of the Russian Princess Fedora in in the eponymous theatrical work written by Frenchman Victorien Sardou. As part of her costume, Bernhardt, who loved to dress in a decidedly masculine manner, wore this soft, wide-brimmed hat—which later came to be known as the Fedora—cocked at an angle over her forehead. An interesting fact if one considers that in an age such as ours, with its debates on gender bending, the fedora is still used by some men, particularly actors, as a fashion statement through which to assert their strong sense of masculinity. Recent television series like *Mad Men* or *Boardwalk Empire* have brought back powerful men, who in their nostalgic revival of older styles—particularly in their use of hats—deeply re-entrench the boundaries of masculinity. And it is along this line that we need to read the historical trajectory of the hat from object to icon. We must clarify a technical point from the outset. The styles considered here are the fedora and the panama, that is, ones that have covered the history of our century while being inextricably linked to the history of a company that later became synonymous with them: Borsalino.

109 Jean-Paul Belmondo and Alain Delon together during the shooting of the film *Borsalino*. The two played Paul Carbone and François Spirito, prominent gangsters in the underworld of Marseilles in the 1930s.

110   Theodore Roosevelt with his legendary white hat during the construction of the Panama Canal in 1907.

The age of the testimonial still lay far in the future when Theodore Roosevelt was photographed in a white hat with a black band, shielding his face from the sun, at one end of the as-of-yet unfinished Panama Canal. That hat, made in Ecuador from Carludovica palm leaves, caught the attention of Giuseppe Borsalino, a tailor from Alessandria, who understood the value of an elegant item that evoked the refinement of a colonial life among banana plantations and aged rum, and began having it shipped by the hundreds from the city of Montecristi, turning it into an object coveted by men all over the world. Borsalino began producing them in 1857; by the outbreak of World War I, its annual output had increased from circa 750,000 to over 2 million pieces, which were exported across the globe. The business' incredible growth managed to astound a company as historically renowned as Stetson, the real giant of the hat industry before the rise of the Piedmont firm.

111 left A group of workers in a Stetson factory wrestling with the mold, one of the most important steps in the production of a hat. Thanks to steam, the felt can be fashioned by hand on the selected mold: the creation of the hat begins at this stage.

111 right A finished hat after a long production process. This Stetson Stratoliner is probably the most iconic model within American tradition, and is also the one that long competed with Borsalino for the market.

112 top A worker busy trimming the brim of a hat to give it the desired breadth. Each step in the process is extremely delicate so as to avoid damaging the fabric in any way; for this reason the workers at Borsalino are highly specialized.

112 bottom Two of the Borsalino styles most in demand by fans worldwide. The packaging is an important step in the process since it's the way in which the finished product is presented to the customer.

With a workforce of 2,500, Borsalino became the symbol of Alessandria, its city of origin, as well as one of the most important industrial firms in Italy. Much has been said about the importance of the cinema in the dissemination and definition of styles and fashion icons, which in this case too has played a key role. At least four movies have the word "Borsalino" in their title and have thus bestowed a heretofore unheard of blessing on this accessory. In 1970, Jacques Deray directed Jean-Paul Belmondo and Alain Delon in *Borsalino*, a story of two outlaws in the 1930s, but above all one of male friendship, which was followed in 1974 by *Borsalino and Co.* By the 1970s, therefore, the hat had acquired such fame that it inspired the names of movies, and was not only an article of clothing and protection but also—and even more so—a polyvalent accessory that spoke about the person wearing it. In *Casablanca*, Humphrey Bogart definitely marked a turning point in the image of the Borsalino, as did *The Godfather*; from there it passed from the adventurous character played by Harrison Ford in Indiana Jones to the ethnic one played by Johnny Depp, who also wears one in private life. Somewhere between fiction and reality, the Borsalino versions of the fedora and the panama typify for the most part of today's imagination. Borsalino's success is the result of the quality, uniqueness, and craftsmanship of the actual product.

113 A wing of the historic Borsalino factory in Alessandria, where the workers are busy using appropriate steel and iron tools for molding hats.

The panama, created in 1835, is made of plant fibers of the *Carludovica* palm through a process that can last up to six months. A journey that began in Ecuador and went on to conquer the Americas and Europe. A story that Borsalino transformed into a timeless legend, which, over the years, became synonymous with elegance. The fedora is crafted from felt made of fine fur (rabbit or hare). It is the manufacturing process—which requires fifty steps and an average of seven weeks of labor per headpiece—that grants the product its unique quality. A process—by now well established—that consists of tiny steps and crucial details, and that is passed down from generation to generation.

115 top Ecuadorian workers collecting and sorting the leaves of the Carludovica palm, used in the manufacture of Panama hats. Only the leaves of this palm are used in an authentic Panama.

115 bottom Two of the best known Panama styles: the classic Borsalino (right), and the Colonial (left). The second is the original type worn by the colonizers who conquered Central America in the 17th century.

As Antonio Gamba relates in his *Manuale del dettagliante cappellaio* [*The Hat Merchant's Manual*] of 1942, "The felt hat differs from any other article of clothing in that it is constituted of a single piece of fabric, which is gradually transformed into a perfect product that covers a man's head." The Gamba family have headed the Panizza label ever since its founder, Giovanni Panizza, handed it over to them nearly a century ago. Since 1879, the firm has focussed on its distinctive workmanship in order to nurture the myth of the most famous men's hat in the world. Everything revolves around the felt. Once the fur has been blended and blown, it can undergo the felting process, which is complete once it has attained its form and size. The shaping of the cone in the felting machine is the key step in the manufacture of the hat. Shaping, hooping, shaving, decorating, and packaging are the essential steps that define its value but also the uniqueness of every single piece. First, steam heat is used to mold the fibers; then, once the head portion is finished, the brim is shaped by pressing and drying in order to prepare the hat for shaving, which is done with shark skin. The band tied with a bow, the lining and the leather that fastens the hat are added last, and all is then carefully packaged.

But every true fan of a fedora or panama knows that there is a sixth step, which never appears in technical manuals, and that is its use. Every had "settles" over time, adjusting to head features in a reciprocal osmosis between person and object. The position occupied by the Borsalino hat in the list of fashion icons is thus firmly sealed, confirmed by time, even if in more recent years the accessory has fallen a bit out of everyday use. But it is once again from Italy that a final—though perhaps not the final—gasp of the style reemerges in the ambiguous character of Jep Gambardella in *The Great Beauty*, who, wearing a panama hat, states: "I'm a gentleman, that's the only thing I know for sure."

116 Molding is the first and possibly most decisive phase in hat production. Form and style are conferred at this point thanks to an iron mold, which imposes the desired shape on the hot fabric.

117 top From the original model to date, the Fedora has undergone many variations in size, height, breadth of brim, or, in a more strictly aesthetic sense, the color combination color of hat and band. The unique quality of each Panizza is guaranteed by Léon, the logo depicting the Jack Russel Terrier, the company's mascot.

117 bottom Panama Panizza styles: the Cuenca Chemise, a tobacco-colored Trilby, and the Colonial.

TUXEDO

SIMPLY CHIC

So great is the importance of the tuxedo to the male wardrobe that it is regarded as the sign of a man's style. At one moment of the tuxedo's greatest popularity, when the legend of Hollywood was on the rise and the 1950s were celebrating stardom, Frank Sinatra used to say that in his mind the tuxedo was not merely a garment but also a lifestyle. Although today this sounds very strange, it will become easier to understand once we go over its history. The tuxedo is definitely one of the most controversial items in men's fashion. Its history, mythical status, and allure fall between England and the United States, where it was submitted to a series of uses, modifications, and legends that made it fluctuate in value over the decades, and thus turned it more than any other garment into an indicator of change in conventions and society. In 1886, the future King Edward VII, still Prince of Wales at the time, asked his tailor and friend Henry Poole of the historical firm Henry Poole & Co. of Savile Row, to shorten the tail of a classic men's coat and create a "dinner jacket," that is, a garment that could be worn to dinner or on informal occasions, and was simply more comfortable. That same year, American millionaire James Brown Potter, who had been introduced to the prince during a trip to England, brought the already popular jacket to America, where he wore it to the annual ball held by an exclusive country club in Tuxedo Park, north of New York City.

119 Like other actors who have played Agent 007, Roger Moore wears a stylish custom-made tuxedo.

We say this with all due respect to those who credit the birth of the tuxedo to Pierre Lorillard and his son Griswold, the Scrooge of all Scrooges of the late nineteenth-century American Tobacco industry. That garment joined Prince Edward's demand for comfort, on the one hand, with the rigid formality of the past, on the other.

The jacket came in different models: single- or double-breasted, with either a peak or a shawl collar, lapels in silk or grosgrain, with or without a vest. The legs of the trousers fell straight down to the shoe, with no cuffs, and had a stripe of the same fabric as the jacket's lapels running down their side. The shirt was white with a jeweled plastron and buttons, the socks black and below the knee, and the shoes black patent-leather Oxfords, or at most a pair of Tuxedo slippers.

The sash was optional, but when present, had to be of the same fabric as the jacket's lapels. The new version of the tailcoat soon supplanted the traditional one and asserted itself as a new classic. All the same, it seems that nothing conveys elegance and sartorial tradition better than the tuxedo does. We have now reached the Roaring Twenties, when Fred Astaire was the epitome of men's style in the new century.

120 Satin lapels, tiny black buttons, bow tie and striped plastron. Another basic component of the tuxedo is the double-cuffed white piqué shirt.

In the 1930s, the tuxedo with a white jacket came to its own. Initially used only in the warm season, it had such an impact on the aesthetic that by the 1950s it too became a classic for any time of year or occasion—as demonstrated by a famous photo of John F. Kennedy and Dwight D. Eisenhower at a White House dinner with Pakistani President Ayub Khan in 1961.

121 1961 was a historical year. John F. Kennedy entered the White House and the politics of the United States and the entire West underwent a radical change. In the 1960s, tuxedos in black or white were worn by politicians on various occasions.

By these years, the language of the movies and swing was spoken all over the world. The new idols in the late 1950s were Frank Sinatra, Dean Martin, Sammy Davis Jr., Peter Lawford, and Joey Bishop, who formed the now famous "Rat Pack," as Lauren Bacall called them. Even a star as far beyond rules as Paul Newman wore the tuxedo. A 1963 photo of him in Venice reveals how this article of dress was capable of transforming even a beauty as savage as Newman's into one of sophisticated elegance. In short, whether at a political ceremony or an evening at the Apollo Theater, success was being measured by the tuxedo. Times change, and certainly no one would have bet on the stamina of the tuxedo in the 1970s.

122 Frank Sinatra and Sammy Davis Jr. joke during a charity dinner in 1961. By the 1950s the tuxedo had become a classic for any event or season.

123 "When they say, 'take off your glasses, I want to see your blue eyes,' I get as mad as a beast," Paul Newman told Oriana Fallaci in 1963 during an interview in Venice for the screening of *Hud*.

Youthful radicalism tore everything deemed a classic into shreds. Nonetheless, in those years nightlife bestowed immortality on the tuxedo. Tony Manero wore an all-white one with a black shirt. The generation of revolutionaries retained its silhouette while drastically altering everything else with soft enormous bow ties, brightly colored jackets, and even fantastically ruffled shirts. The tuxedo became an icon, indestructible and versatile enough to survive the storm of the seventies, proving itself to be an article of dress that demanded confrontation. Tom Ford tried restoring it to its original form, though with slight updates. "A man in a tuxedo can also be sexy," the designer from Texas has claimed. A statement of epic proportions. Today the tuxedo is a passe-partout. From ceremonies to the red carpet, even the less worldly man has one in his closet. Today's stars have revitalized it. Constrained by protocol to wearing it, they have begun playing around with a seemingly stagnant item. Thus from the Brioni tuxedo worn for decades by James Bond, we move on to the allure of new idols. Most likely aided by the worldwide popularity of Mad Men, certain types of formal attire are back in fashion, and the tuxedo is once again taking the lion's share. With his knowing elegance and innate charm, George Clooney is surely one of the best modern interpreters of this historical garment. Far more original are the interpretations given it by Jared Leto and Pharrell Williams, who have worn the suit with shorts, or Neil Patrick Harris, who has worn it in every color save black, much like Kevin Spacey, who made his appearance on the red carpet in an electric blue version. Adrien Brody's languid looks grant it a decidedly dandyish quality.

124 Beautiful, bold, and Texan. Early in his designer career the still unknown Tom Ford had no experience with the selective world of fashion. Soon, however, he proved to have very clear things to say about glamor, success, and style, bringing back an allure in the 1970s that seemed to have been buried.

125 top Joking, George Clooney states a truism: "Unfortunately, you can't regulate good taste." That's because his appearance is always impeccable. Many great fashion figures, such as Giorgio Armani, have continually provided him with suits, including tuxedos.

125 bottom The process of constructing the image of a star extends to every action and every choice. It may seem simplistic, but even the color of a tuxedo worn at a media event as important as the Oscars speaks of the role that an actor such as Kevin Spacey chooses to play within stardom.

126 and 127 The tuxedo, dinner jacket, or "smoking jacket"—as in the term *smoking*, the word used to denote this garment in Italian—all refer to the dressing gown, since the activities that noble lords engaged in while wearing such jackets were typical of domestic leisure.

The final affront—or variation, depending on one's point of view—has come from fashion designers. Most famous is Dolce & Gabbana's version with a T-shirt and torn jeans, proposed both for the runway and everyday usage. The true nature of the tuxedo actually lies in the highly flexible duplicity of a code that fluctuates between form and personality. When the manner of wearing a certain item prevails over formal rules, it becomes timeless. American fashion reporter George Hamilton explains this well in the words of a former downtown Manhattan clothing store's owner: "In the end, it doesn't even matter whether it is well made or not. You have to wear it with the familiarity of an unmade bed. You have to wear it in a formal way, but do so as though you had gotten dressed in the dark. Grab the clutch without looking in the mirror. This is how a tuxedo will get you everywhere."

128-129 Grand finale to the beat of a tuxedo. The stylistic code of this clothing item is so powerful and iconic that it can be used even in the most extreme fashion. Bent on rewriting the masculine code of dress, Dolce & Gabbana propose a wardrobe without any rules, yet dictated by the fusion of absolutely opposing elements.

PAJAMA

GENTLEMEN MAKING COMFORTABLE

The right pajamas can confer timeless elegance on a man's wardrobe. If a person's style can be intuited from details, then these are definitely an indicator. Intimate occasions relegated to the night or relaxing ones that occur during free time could grant every man the freedom to treat "night wear" in a rudimentary, even slovenly fashion. A stylish man, however, puts as much care into these items as he does into his entire wardrobe. I speak in the plural, because in addition to pajamas there is at least one other article of demans that demands to be discussed here: the bathrobe. The pajama is probably the only garment that goes by the same name around the world. This speaks well of its great success since the late nineteenth century, when the English appropriated it from Indian culture during the colonial era. The word derives from the Hindi *pajāmā*, which, in turn, had its origin in the Persian *pāy jamè*, meaning a garment for the legs. Originally pajamas consisted of a pair of very soft and full trousers, loosely bound at the waist. English officials began using them in the torrid months in order to be more comfortable and to combat the heat and humidity of the Indian continent. Realizing their practicality, they continued to wear them even after they returned to their homeland; it was from there that they spread like wildfire throughout the West. A relationship that we might call confidential was soon established with the garment—above all in Anglo-Saxon countries, where it came to be known by various nicknames such as PJs, jim-jams, or jammies.

131 James Stewart in a scene from the movie *Rear Window*. Alfred Hitchcock's absolute masterpiece was presented at the Venice International Film Festival in 1954.

By the 1920s, it was a key element in our daily lives. The original style consisted of two pieces, a jacket and trousers, made from silk or high-quality cotton. The fabrics were primarily those used for shirts, either striped or in pastel hues. In this case too, film and television contributed not a little to the garment's success. On the one hand, they offered the reassuring image of the family of the 1950s, in which sons and fathers found themselves on a bed or couch dressed in the same pajamas as in scenes from *The Sound of Music*, on the other, they presented them as a symbol of perfect aplomb irrespective of circumstances, as in the case of James Stewart in Hitchcock's *Rear Window* of 1954, or of Montgomery Clift, portrayed in bed while reading the *New Yorker* in more or less the same years. Surely the greatest representative of the male sex in these decades was James Bond, the leading proponent of traditional masculinity when it came to upbringing and provenance, but absolutely modern when it came to lifestyle. We find interesting examples of the use of pajamas in the various episodes in which he appeared—from the stripped down version made of ethereal foam worn by Sean Connery, to Roger Moore's sexy robe in *Octopussy*. In 1958, the same charm, though darker, was exuded by Paul Newman, who wore pajamas and a bathrobe through nearly an entire movie while starring opposite Elizabeth Taylor in *Cat on a Hot Tin Roof*, or by Marlon Brando in several scenes of *A Streetcar Named Desire*. These decades were an important period for the acceptance of pajamas and associated garments. Looking through the many movie productions of the time, we come up with other examples. Thus we find Rock Hudson wandering in his pajamas through a garden in *Send Me No Flowers*. Yet their indubitable success does not end there. Our collective imagination is full of famous stars flaunting their pajamas, especially in recent decades. It begins with Warren Beatty, who had himself photographed dressed solely in pajama bottoms in the hallways of a hotel, testifying to an utterly 1970s audacity—a bit in the way that years later James Franco posted a selfie of himself wearing embarrassing pajamas in a baby print. Thus began what was practically a game both on and off the screen. Some like Johnny Depp in *The Tourist* or Quentin Tarantino in his cameo appearance in *Pulp Fiction*, which he directed, or Jeff Bridges in *The Big Lebowski* have turned them into a nearly existential and alternative symbol, stripping them of their former "stylish" appeal. Other people in show business have worn them to events, propelling them for all intents and purposes to the level of fashion. In an age in which the watchwords of menswear are ever more frequently "casual," "relaxed," and "comfortable," pajamas have become the mantra of a new aesthetic. This is conveyed by Robert Pattinson, the current new idol, half-awake on the stairs of his home, beer in hand, and dressed in pajamas after a night of partying with friends, or by Orlando Bloom, who pairs them with an oversized coat, and equally by Ryan Gosling and Woody Harrelson, who wore them on the red carpet at Cannes and at the premiere of *Hunger Games*.

132 Montgomery Clift or "Monty," as he was affectionately nicknamed, was one of the most beloved American actors of the 1950s. There are very few photos of him in his private life.

Perhaps their success is also indebted to fashion runways; Dolce & Gabbana, for example, recently bestowed the blessings of glamor on the garment. Setting aside top-notch designers, however, other smaller firms have turned pajamas into their key strength. The classic of classics is located in London. Derek Rose is one of the oldest and finest manufacturers of high-end pajamas, so much so that it finds itself on the "golden mile" of Savile Row, next to highly prestigious tailors. Other internationally renowned brands include Hanro and Zimmerli, as well as menswear shrines such as Brooks Brothers or Ralph Lauren. Nevertheless, two companies must be mentioned alongside these giants. The first is Olatz, a line created by Julian Schnabel's ex-wife in 2003 and inspired precisely by those worn by the American artist. Due to his size, Schnabel began using a classic type of silk pajama with hemmed borders, which he usually wore beneath his coat as if it were a suit.

134 The final runway at the Dolce & Gabbana fashion show, which proposed the pajama as the principal clothing item of Winter 2016.

135 top Derek Rose has been manufacturing pajamas since 1927. The company can truly be deemed a "heritage brand" as it has now been managed by the same family for four generations.

135 bottom left "Understated Luxury" has been Hanro's motto for over 130 years. By now the Swiss brand has become an international cult.

135 bottom right Most Olatz pajamas are made in Madeira, a Portuguese island famous for its artisanal goods.

The second is an all-Italian company, yet known among fans and pajama lovers well beyond the nation's borders: Loretta Caponi, an artisanal company in Florence that has been manufacturing top-quality garments and supplying heads of state and celebrities from around the world for decades.

136 Since 1967 Loretta Caponi created high-quality men's pajamas, combining classical style with typical Italian creativity, especially in the choice of fabrics.

137 A Zimmerli model in piped silk. The Swiss company has been manufacturing all its items in Coldrerio since 1965. Production continues to increase steadily, thanks to an extremely effective export policy.

POLO SHIRT

WHEN SPORTS DO STYLE

It's not difficult to become an icon when you're a revolution's leading figure. Indeed, as often happens, the simplest ideas, those that arise from everyday needs, risk becoming mass and at times even ironic phenomena. This has been the case with the polo shirt, which at the age of nearly one hundred is more youthful and vital than ever before, to the degree that it seems to have no rivals. Jean-René Lacoste fiddled around with the formal attire used by tennis players at the beginning of the century in order to increase freedom of movement. Thus arose the modern polo shirt and a new chapter in men's fashion in the early years of the twentieth century. In those times, sports shirts had long sleeves and buttoned collars to provide enough space for the ties that were worn even on the court. Lacoste designed a more functional alternative: a short-sleeved T-shirt in breathable cotton piqué with a soft collar that could be buttoned up with only two buttons on the chest. On it, he applied an image of a little crocodile, since reporters of the era had nicknamed him "the Crocodile." René Lacoste himself spoke about this: "The U.S. press nicknamed me 'the Crocodile' after I made a bet with the Captain of the French team at the Davis Cup.

139 From the beginning, Lacoste's marketing was keenly aware of the versatility of its principal item. In this 1933 ad, the polo shirt is portrayed in a tennis court, but in a way to suggest its use even at moments of leisure.

He promised to get me a crocodile-skin suitcase if I won an important match for the team. The American public remembered this nickname, which underscored my tenacity on the tennis court since I never let go of my prey! My friend Robert George drew a little crocodile for me, which I later had embroidered on the blazer that I wore on the court." The episode is particularly interesting because this was the first garment in history to display a logo, inadvertently initiating a phenomenon that fashion later turned into logomania. Lacoste got the idea for this shirt from another clothing item already used by polo players (hence the name), a sport successfully imported from the region of ancient Persia at the very beginning of the century. Soon to become the favorite sport of the English aristocracy, polo helped introduce and spread the garment as a fashion item. It was no accident, in fact, that it was used in the two most elegant sports of the period. It was thus that in 1933, 7 years after his debut on the tennis court, René Lacoste along with his friend André Gillier founded the company Chemise Lacoste, through which they marketed the product all over the world. Although the word "classic" is often used too generously in men's fashion, it is nonetheless true that there's no better term for describing the role that this shirt has played in the history of apparel. In the nearly one hundred years of its existence, the polo has not changed at all and has gotten through the decades unharmed. Instantly an icon of casual and informal apparel, the polo soon demonstrated its full versatility by also inserting itself into the more formal areas of menswear. Its iconic style was so apparent and obvious from the outset that in the same years that the Lacoste company was being founded, other firms arose and took over a sector of the clothing industry.

140 The original polo shirt was called L.12.12 by its creator: L stood for Lacoste; 1 for the unique petit piqué fabric; 2 for its two short sleeves; and 12 for the number of versions designed by René.

141 In addition to being a formidable tennis player, René Lacoste was also an inventor and a great businessman. He used to present his new styles to his son and collaborators in his historic studio.

Fred Perry, another famous tennis player (the first Englishman to win Wimbeldon), along with former Austrian soccer player Tibby Wegner, launched their venture with the laurel-wreath label. The tremendous popular success of the Fred Perry polo owed much to the culture of the Mods, who adopted and combined it with other clothing items, thereby endowing them with an anti-conformist charm that they still lacked. The 1960s, in fact, debunked the aristocratic image and snob appeal that the polo had earned for itself up until that moment. In turn, an image of the preppy boy that had been nurtured by American college culture lay behind the success of at least two other firms that were closely bound to this clothing item.

142 Fred Perry, a man of many records, was an unparalleled champion who represented the image of the English courts worldwide. He was the first to win Wimbledon for three consecutive years (1934-1936), the first to win all four titles of the Grand Slam, and also helped England win the Davis Cup four years in a row, from 1933 to 1936.

143 The Fred Perry polo is the iconic item of one of the most important clothing companies in the U.K. Adopted by the Mods in the 1950s, it soon caught the interest of international fashion. Many designers, including Raf Simons, have collaborated with this brand, creating either entire lines or simply improving particular details of the shirt.

143

In 1896, after a trip to Britain, John E. Brooks, the founder of Brooks Brothers, added the polo uniform's collar detail to his shirts in order to create the original polo shirt, that is, the cotton piqué button-down shirt that later became identified with the American brand. Long afterwards, in 1972, Ralph Lauren (né Ralph Lifschitz), designed a new line of apparel around this garment, which he simply named Polo, thereby ordaining its status as an icon once and for all.

144 Leonardo DiCaprio wearing a Ralph Lauren polo shirt on the set of the movie *The Wolf of Wall Street*.

Speaking of tennis, an Italian too scored a major victory in the history of the polo shirt: Sergio Tacchini. In the 1970s and 1980s, great tennis champions like McEnroe and Connors only wore the Tacchini polo shirt, thus promoting its international reputation. This was the same item with a few minor add-ons: two branded buttons, elasticized wrists (especially in the long-sleeved version), and two unmistakable stripes—the distinctive sign of the brand. Thus over time, moving between Europe and the United States, the polo became an integral feature of any and every wardrobe. From a stylistic point of view, it was in fact regarded as a valid solution for all those occasions that did not require formal wear but were also not completely casual.

145 The first real tennis stars were athletes such as John McEnroe, who wore Sergio Tacchini. It was for this reason that the Italian brand became the undisputed leader on tennis courts in the 1970s and 1980s.

Short- or long-sleeved, with jeans or formal slacks, in various fabrics and a nearly infinite range of colors, the polo shirt can be paired with anything. That's the key to its success. No classification system can force the polo shirt into a single category. In his family photos (on a boat or in a vacation home) John F. Kennedy, standing in for America's bourgeois elite, reinstated the polo shirt's typically sophisticated but relaxed appeal. Clint Eastwood, always the epitome of the rugged male, used it to maintain a certain distance between himself and the image imposed on him by fame, wearing it with classic pleated trousers and a jacket over his shoulder. Japanese actor Toshirō Mifune had himself photographed in Venice in the 1960s looking like Cary Grant in *Roman Holiday*, while Terence Stamp, wearing it with a pair of jeans and a few accessories, tried, like all Englishmen, to give it back a mood somewhere between shabby and chic. Everyone can have his own idea on how to exploit the polo shirt's adaptability, its precarious perch between formality and informality. Even the simple act of wearing it tucked into slacks or hanging out can make a difference.

The rapper prefers the sporty side of the polo shirt; indeed in 2000 Kanye West fell so deeply in love with it that he turned it practically into a uniform, choosing to wear ones by Ralph Lauren and Tommy Hilfiger. In *The Wolf of Wall Street*, on the other hand, the yuppy Jordan Belfort was more inclined to wear the polo shirt in an impeccable manner, as much during leisure hours as when doing business. Its fame has thus grown so great over time as to render it immune from any rules of style, impervious to every norm. Actually it's not the polo shirt that is versatile; it's the other menswear items that must change their nature to adapt themselves to this one, which, immutable, is always equal to itself.

146 Toshirō Mifune in casual clothes at the Venice Film Festival in the 1960s.

147 In America, the concept of elite is represented by great bourgeois families such as the Kennedys, who convey the idea of a totally comfortable and relaxed elegance.

SUNGLASSES

AT FIRST GLANCE

It is immediately obvious that mental processes and psychological motives that transcend fashion lie behind the use of eyeglasses. One could bring up great literary figures such as Aldous Huxley or Marshall McLuhan, who in the *Art of Seeing* (1943) and *Understanding Media* (1964), respectively, confer philosophical meaning on eyeglasses, the "infernal logic" of which "forces eyes into a state of rigid structural immobility. Actually, the success of glasses is as always indebted to sociological dynamics bound to aesthetics and far more basic psychological processes. The philosophy of sunglasses transcends by far the significance of an accessory that first and foremost makes us hip, as Vanessa Brown has rightly recounted in her book *Cool Shades* (2014) Their shape instantly grants the face a new symmetry or else enhances the one that it already possesses. The inductive method that we test on a daily basis, that lets us understand through trial and error whether or not something is good, places sunglasses among those things that we always carry around with us. If we leave the house sloppily dressed because we're in a rush or due to carelessness, putting on a pair of shades will cancel every stylistic gaffe. It's as though glasses help us be less visible to the world and the center of attention simultaneously; they enhance our face by drawing attention away from its imperfections.

149 In 1978 Dan Aykroyd and John Belushi founded the The Blues Brothers band in order to perform a skit in an episode of *Saturday Night Live*. Their image has become permanently associated with Ray-Bans.

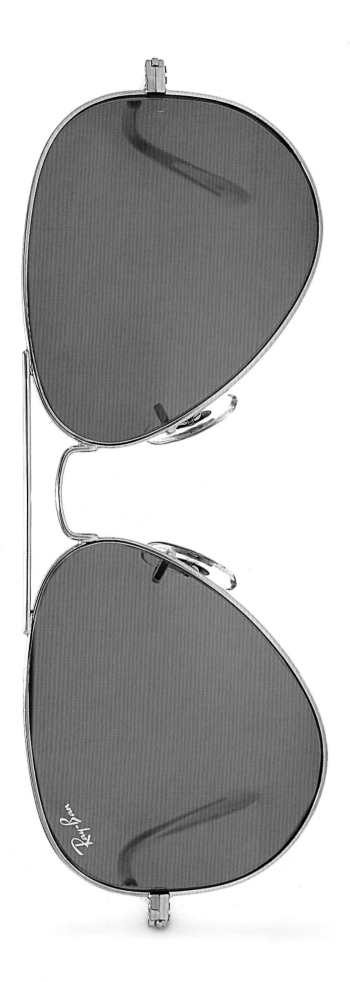

Then too there's the power of mystery, the sense of detachment and vulnerability. If judgment is shaped above all through the eyes (a medium that enables us to communicate reliability, security, depth, and intention), then wearing sunglasses shields us from the gaze of others but also deprives us of our power to express. Perhaps this is the "rigid immobility" of which Huxley spoke in his book. Or perhaps in this case we should seek support from Erving Goffman, who in *The Presentation of Self in Everyday Life* speaks of the dynamics that lie at the basis of eye contact between strangers, which he sums up as "civil inattention." For Goffman, life is a theater, or better yet, lots of theaters, and each one of us plays multiple roles. After scrutinizing each other from afar, two strangers who meet on the street tend to avert their eyes in order to "make it clear to the other that he or she is not a special object of aesthetic or curious interest." Sunglasses can change this dynamic as they no longer require that the gaze—harnessed as it is behind lenses—be averted. But while continuing down the psycho-sociological route that explains the accessory's allure, we must speak of the many iconic moments that glasses—as both a corrective tool and symbol of charm and mystery—have provided us in little more than 50 years. In 1981 the famous Sicilian singer-songwriter Franco Battiato sang: "There are those who wears sunglasses to be more charismatic and imply a mystery." And though this was a shrewd attempt at irony directed at excessive and at times uncalled for use of sunglasses, it hit home. The pairing of charm and mystery has always exerted a strong influence on individuals—especially when associated with celebrities, who from the 1950s onwards contributed significantly to their success.

The American brand Ray-Ban, which began by creating glasses to satisfy military needs—to protect U.S. Air Force pilots from the blinding light of the sun—asserted itself in the decades when the accessory was catching on. Then a new type of eyeglasses with green lenses that were capable of eliminating reflection without obscuring vision was introduced. Thus arose Ray-Bans. The original style, universally known as Aviators, consisted of a classic frame in plastic with teardrop-shaped rims; the next year the frame came out in metal and was renamed "Ray-Ban Aviators." Soon the popularity of Ray-Bans spread from a limited circle of pilots to all those who loved life out of doors. In 1938, Ray-Ban launched the Shooter, available either with green or light yellow Kalichrome lenses, which, by filtering out blue light, made it possible to see details more sharply under hazy conditions and minimized the impact of fog. The Ray-Ban Outdoorsman came out the following year. Initially called "Skeet Glasses" and made for hunting, fishing, and shooting buffs, these glasses had a top bar and earpieces made of various materials, such as mother-of-pearl and calfskin. By this point, U.S. Air Force pilots only placed their trust in Ray-Bans. Research and development led to interesting inventions, above all mirrored sunglasses with a special coating on the upper portion of the lens to maximize protection and none on the bottom to ensure clearer vision of the airplane's dashboard. Although they were designed for military use, Ray-Ban products and innovations also appealed to ordinary people. In those years, military heroes like General Douglas MacArthur were genuine role models; however, with the growing success of the film industry, they were soon supplanted by actors. In the 1950s, sunglasses, along with T-shirts, marked a sharp generational rift; James Dean wore Ray-Ban Wayfarers in *Rebel Without a Cause* (1955), Bob Dylan wore them at many concerts, while Peter Fonda chose Ray-Ban Olympians in *Easy Rider* (1969). Of course, if we're talking about coolness we have to proceed to the 1980s, but a bit earlier there were two cinematic moments of great visual and social impact: in 1971, Clint Eastwood sported a pair of Baloramas in *Dirty Harry*, while in 1976, Robert De Niro wore a pair of Caravans in *Taxi Driver*. If in the cases cited thus far, glasses played a supporting role to profound characters such as Travis Bickle, after 1980 they took the lead.

150 The frames known as Large Metal, and later as Aviators, were designed in the laboratories of Bausch & Lomb in 1920 at the request of General John Macready, but were not patented until 1937.

151 Bob Dylan in a pair of Ray-Ban Wayfarer plays the harmonica before a microphone during the recording of his album *Bringing It All Back Home*.

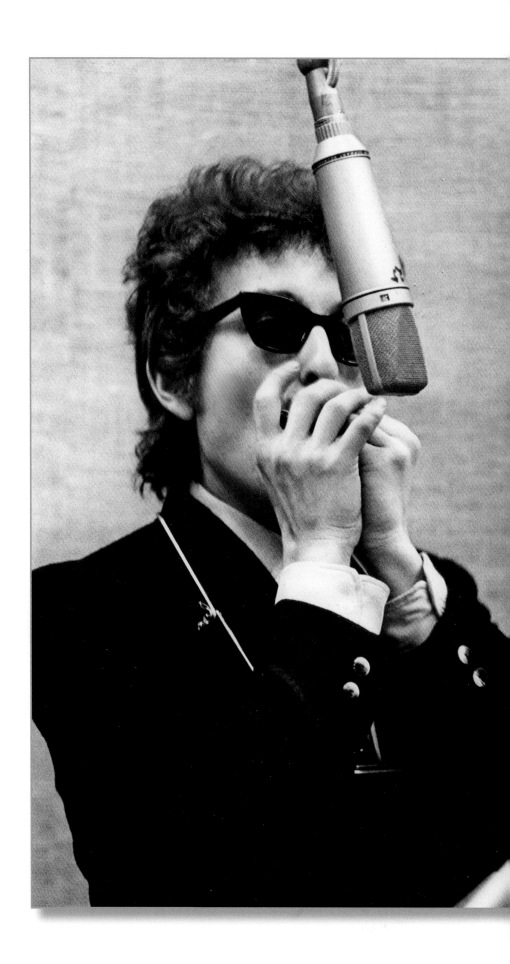

152 Justice as represented by Inspector Callaghan has always been characteristic of the nation of stars and stripes. "Dirty Harry," as the inspector was called, was a trigger-happy cop always in formal attire and a pair of Baloramas.

153 In the epoch-making 1969 road movie *Easy Rider*, Peter Fonda chose a pair of Olympians when playing his character.

154 Ray-Bans also lend themselves to irony and fun. In *Men In Black*, Will Smith derides those who take themselves too seriously, hiding alleged seriousness and excessive concern behind a pair of black shades.

It's impossible not to think about the stars of *The Blues Brothers* without recollecting the black Wayfarers they wore throughout the film, or about Tom Cruise in his Aviators and all his cool glamorous charm in *Top Gun* of 1986. Those same years Michael Jackson wore Aviators to the Grammy Award ceremony (1984), and Wayfarers throughout his Bad Tour. Legends do not arise from a unique initial act but from a layering of factors that make them timeless. For this reason there are other highly iconic moments in which sunglasses tell a story with a leading character. That was the case with Denzel Washington's Ray-Ban Clubmasters in *Malcolm X* of 1992 or Tim Roth in Tarantino's *Reservoir Dogs* (1992), or more recently Will Smith and Tommy Lee Jones with their Predators in *Men in Black* (1997), or Johnny Depp's character Raoul Duke in *Fear and Loathing in Las Vegas* (1998). Ray-Bans are such a legend that *Time* magazine ranked them alongside Coca-Cola and Harley-Davidson in their list of American symbols.

155 The visionary Terry Gilliam leads Benicio del Toro and Johnny Depp in a hallucinatory adventure in America's most delirious city—Las Vegas. With his Ray-Ban Shooters, the protagonist Raoul Duke plays a warped character of the contemporary Far West.

However, in the 1940s a competitor arose in Italy that in time cut into Ray-Ban's monopoly: this was Persol, a company founded by Giuseppe Ratti in 1938 to pioneer quality and fit. Its success came with the 649 model designed to protect streetcar conductors in Turin from the environment and dust. The design was so innovative that it spread immediately, thanks again to the support of the movie industry. In 1961, Marcello Mastroianni wore a pair in *Divorce Italian Style*, and later, in 1968, Steve McQueen wore the 714 model in *The Thomas Crown Affair*. Two very different situations. In the true spirit of "Made in Italy", Persol added design and craftsmanship to the prerequisites of utility and coolness, which made the company's glasses highly prized by connoisseurs, especially athletes, over time. Both companies, however, have helped change eyewear from a purely practical accessory to an indispensable item of modern taste.

156 Persol models such as the 649 (center) and Cellor (top), have retained their design over time, occasionally submitting to minor changes, as in the case of the model 714 (bottom), which has evolved over the years into a foldable version.

157 One of the finest films in cinema history, *The Thomas Crown Affair* strangely starred Steve McQueen, one of the least stylish actors in Hollywood. Nevertheless his performance established the fame of both him and his Persols, which he wore throughout the film but also in his private life.

GOMMINO

HISTORY OF AN ICON

The role of the shoe within attire has changed over time from that of a simple accessory to that of a fundamental element of style. Like a synecdoche, the shoe speaks not only of itself or of the foot that it must hold, but of the individual as a whole. The relationship between the shoe and the individual has unexpected socio-cultural implications; it is no longer man who gives form and substance to the shoe (by using it), but the shoe—with its conspicuous display of a designer label and thus the allure of reassuring validation—that defines the person who wears it, that makes the person. The shoe is the means through which every disparity is toned down and the infinite variety of individuals is reduced to a few, easily classifiable categories. Nevertheless, there is one shoe that seems to have taken the opposite route and become famous for prioritizing comfort and recovering the value of utility and craftsmanship. The shoe in question is the driving loafer, or, as it is commonly called, the *gommino* moccasin. This is perhaps one of the few cases of a success that belongs entirely to Italy. The famous "Made in Italy" tag, now the basis for any phenomenon related to fashion and design, frequently refers only to the act of manufacturing—an "upgrade" in terms of quality and design of pre-existing objects or those invented by others. The gommino loafer, on the other hand, is—save for a few details—an utterly Italian story. The moccasin was an object already worn by Native Americans, and probably some version of it similar to the one known today was seen at some point in France.

159 The Car Shoe arose from a patent issued by the Italian Ministry of Industry and Commerce in recognition of the shoe's innovative and original quality.

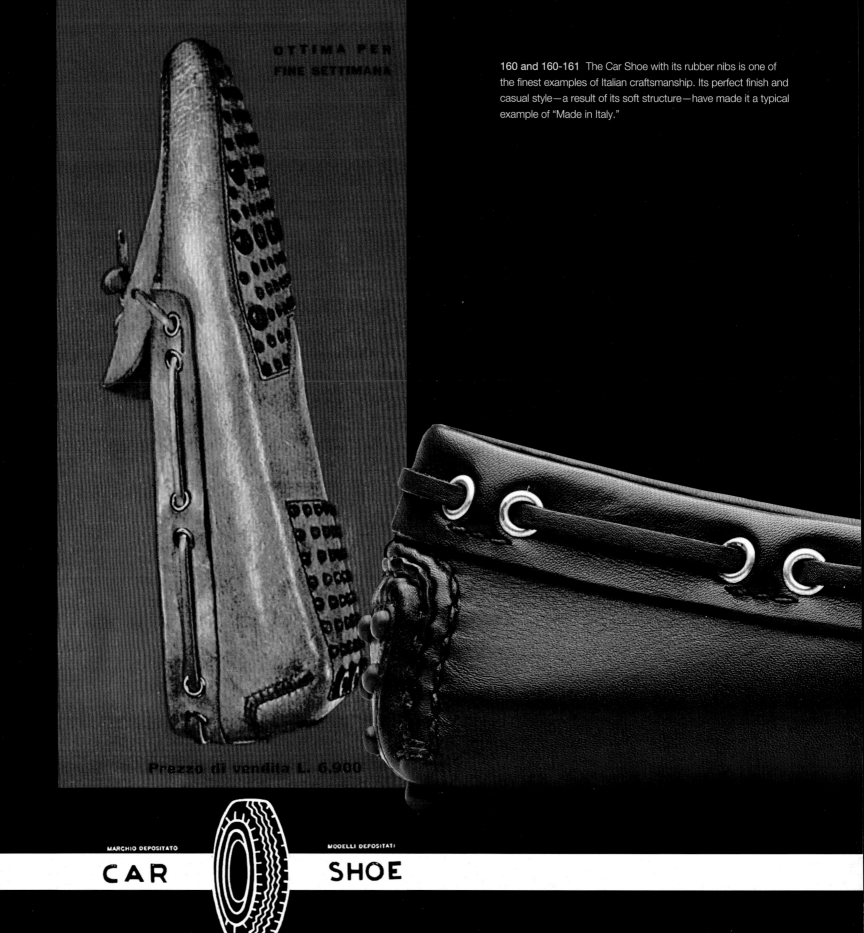

160 and 160-161 The Car Shoe with its rubber nibs is one of the finest examples of Italian craftsmanship. Its perfect finish and casual style—a result of its soft structure—have made it a typical example of "Made in Italy."

But actually it was Gianni Mostile who patented this shoe style in Vigevano in 1963. A huge fan of hand-crafted shoes and motor racing, Mostile intuited that this was the right moment for promoting a totally unstructured moccasin with a sole resting on rubber pellets. This idea made his fortune as well as that of the company that he named "Car Shoe." The shoe seems to have been conceived specifically for those who loved driving, so much so that it was instantly adopted by the international jet set and transformed into a classic menswear item in less than two decades. The first endorsement is said to have come from Gianni Agnelli and after him Onassis, John F. Kennedy, and every driver of a Mercedes, Ferrari, or other big car name associated with Formula One races.

Another, at the time still tiny Italian shoe manufacturer took off on the same track with another style of "driving shoe" that was to enjoy worldwide success and become synonymous with the Italian loafer with the rubber pellet sole: Tod's. In Casette d'Ete in the Marche, Dorino Della Valle created a small shoe company out of a workshop belonging to his father Bernardo Philip, which had produced footwear for brands such as Calvin Klein and Azzedine Alaïa. His son Diego was first sent to study in Bologna. Afterwards, during a trip to New York, legend has it that Diego found an old driver's moccasin and decided to take it home and transform it into an icon. Obviously, there is no way of proving the truth of this tale, but regardless of whether it happened by luck or calculation, the outcome was a genuine success. "While everyone in Italy at the time was drawn to the flashy—recalls Diego Della Valle—I wanted to create a casual product that would be worn with a suit during the week, and with jeans on weekends. That was Tod's brilliant idea, with a key innovative idea: to make the rubber sole elegant." Thus was born the *gommino*, the loafer with 133 pellets. According to Diego Della Valle's account, the company's name was found in the Boston telephone directory: JP Tod was short, effective, and would sound the same all over the world. Afterwards the initials were simply dropped from the surname and the English possessive "s" added. Beyond the rivalry and disputes generated by the question of the gommino's inventor, no one—not even drivers who by now have been wearing them for years—can deny that the two companies raised the driving shoe to the Everest of menswear fashion icons in unbeatable record time. Car Shoe and Tod's have become synonymous with this style of shoe. Much of the loafer's success is attributable to the fact that it is instantly perceived as a luxury item thanks to the use of the finest leather, but above all to the almost entirely artisanal craftsmanship that goes into its creation. Many of the steps can be done solely by hand, and a loafer with rubber pellets requires at least 2-3 hours of manual labor. The Car Shoe, for example, relies on a manual tubular process with 4.85 meters (16 ft) of English twine, the use of rubber pellets that rest atop a rubber base made from a combination of tire treads and 160 hand-sewn stitches that pierce and sew the upper portion of the shoe. We are talking about 100 different steps to create one of Tod's loafers—from the cutting of the fine leather to the hand-stitched assembly of a shoe that requires thirty pieces of leather. From Jack Nicholson to George Clooney, from Orlando Bloom to Antonio Banderas, there is not a single celebrity, not even a businessman, who does not have one or more pairs of gommino loafers in his closet. In the early 1980s, some twenty years after the gommino phenomenon, Italian film director Nanni Moretti observed in *Bianca*: "When I saw his shoes, I understood everything about him. He is a man who has suffered." Car Shoe and Tod's loafers, in contrast, speak of a totally different kind of man: elegant, wealthy, and very comfortable.

162 133 rubber nibs are arranged in a regular pattern on the entire surface of a Tod's sole, so as to offer perfect support for the foot. Thanks to the rubber out of which they are made, they wear very slowly and last for decades.

164 top and 165 To end up as a perfect pair of Tod's, a shoe has to go through many stages. The moment in which the rubber sole meets the vamp is crucial. Once the leather has been cut to the pattern, the holes are made by hand, then the whole thing is assembled.

164 bottom A finished Tod's shoe. The leather is perfectly polished and every detail has been executed with skill and precision.

DENIM

THE DEMOCRACY OF FASHION

I jeans, you jeans, we jeans. It's strange that English has not yet turned the word "jeans" into a verb. In a language that sees its elasticity as a virtue and in which anything can be transformed into a predicate by the simple addition of "to", it is hard to believe that one can say "to Google" but cannot use the expression "to jeans." This certainly remains the one area that blue canvas did not revolutionize. Actually, a linguistic question immediately pops up: blue canvas or denim and jeans are words that mean two different things. Denim is a fabric; jeans are a style of trousers sewn from this fabric. By now, however, the superimposition of one over the other is nearly imperceptible; in its frenetic consumption of expressions and allocutions with which to fill pages and pages of magazines, the language of fashion and costume has diminished the difference in meaning. So much so that we now generally speak of a "denim phenotype" in all its manifestations—pants, shirts, jackets. Denim has quickly become a collective myth bound to the image of celebrities or epochal phenomena of the twentieth century. Certainly the absolute novelty of this fabric, which appeared in the life of American miners in the late 1800s, lies at the basis of its popularity. As often happens, one of the most American icons recognized by pop culture has European origins, and France, Italy, and in some sense Germany can each claim paternity.

167 The forefather of every pair of jeans is the Levi's 501, which has remained essentially unchanged since 1890. Its popularity among fans is due precisely to its fidelity to the original.

In 1853, Levi Strauss, the anglicization of the German Löb Strauß, moved from New York to San Francisco with the conviction that California and the gold rush of the period would be good for the family business, a garment manufacturer. But when he arrived in San Francisco, his clothing shipment had already "sold out" and all he had left was some coarse cloth of the sort used for wagon tarps. This was to be his fortune. From it he cut and fashioned a pair of rugged trousers, which became the joy of a miner in the region who was fed up with wearing garments that always fell apart. These were the first Levi's in history. Thus arose Levi Strauss & Co., which aside from regular clothing items produced pants that soon became very popular among miners, but were in no way similar to those we know today. The first step towards their present form occurred with a change in fabric and the selection of a more comfortable one. Levi opted for denim—a textile originating in the city of Nîmes in France—in blue. Strauss's idea in fact was not new; some decades earlier, the sailors of Genoa had tried to do something similar with fabric used for boat sails, but without the same success.

168 One of the first advertisements of Levi Strauss & Co. proposes a total denim look as the new uniform for all laborers in need of durable and practical clothing.

168-169 Oregon lumberjacks soon adopted the jeans as their favorite garment for their difficult labor. Images such as these are quite common in the late 19th and early 20th century.

The inventiveness of the Italian people, however, did not go unrecognized; a trace of it was retained at least in the name of the Strauss-made trousers: blue jeans, in which the first word obviously refers to the color, while jeans stands for Genes, the word used at the time to refer to the Genoese. Nevertheless it took a tailor from Nevada, Jacob Davis, to take the decisive step towards the creation of the myth. In 1871, Davis added some pockets with copper rivets that prevented them from continuously tearing. This was such an ingenious idea that Davis and Levi applied for a joint patent; thus were born jeans as we know them today. The label also appeared in 1886: a leather tag summing up the quality of the Levi's product—two horses dragging a pair of trousers without ripping them. From that moment on, various by now historically acclaimed brands came into being—Wrangler, Lee, and Rifle—especially after 1908, the year in which Levi lost exclusive rights over the production of jeans. Denim's success as a global clothing item thus had its roots in the United States of America. Soon after being acclaimed as a versatile and rugged garment by miners and farmers, its features affected the more powerful image of America of those years—that of the cowboy, who immediately adopted the jeans as his uniform. By the 1930s, therefore, they had come to represent the quintessence of the traditional American lifestyle with people who were prepared to pay to live the dream of a life on a ranch in the Wild West. Afterwards, the war exported denim, and even Europeans were able to dress like a Yankee. From here on, the timeline that impressed denim onto the collective imagination worldwide passed, as usual, through cinema, then fashion. That which *Time* defined as the "best fashion of the 20th century," was initially to dress Americans at leisure and later to become the recognizable symbol of an entire generation.

170 Today label is synonymous with brand, and Levi's was certainly a forerunner in this regard as well. The first label on its jeans has by now become a cult object as well as the company's image.

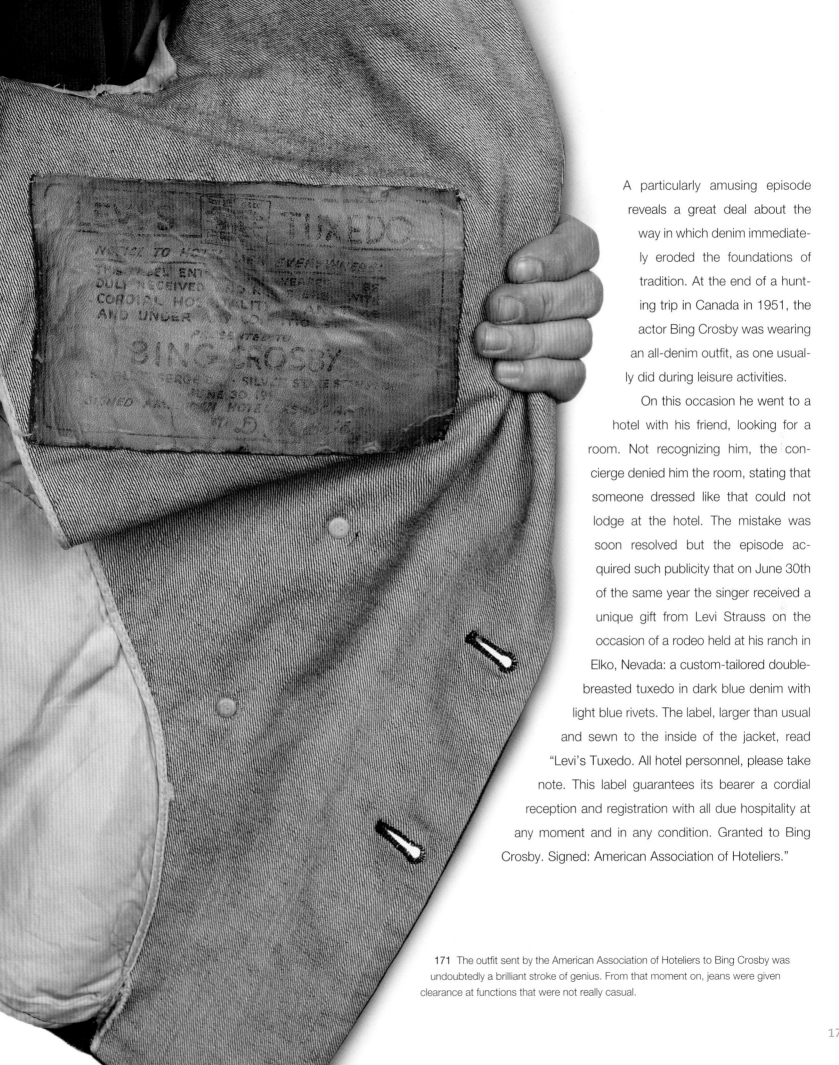

A particularly amusing episode reveals a great deal about the way in which denim immediately eroded the foundations of tradition. At the end of a hunting trip in Canada in 1951, the actor Bing Crosby was wearing an all-denim outfit, as one usually did during leisure activities.

On this occasion he went to a hotel with his friend, looking for a room. Not recognizing him, the concierge denied him the room, stating that someone dressed like that could not lodge at the hotel. The mistake was soon resolved but the episode acquired such publicity that on June 30th of the same year the singer received a unique gift from Levi Strauss on the occasion of a rodeo held at his ranch in Elko, Nevada: a custom-tailored double-breasted tuxedo in dark blue denim with light blue rivets. The label, larger than usual and sewn to the inside of the jacket, read "Levi's Tuxedo. All hotel personnel, please take note. This label guarantees its bearer a cordial reception and registration with all due hospitality at any moment and in any condition. Granted to Bing Crosby. Signed: American Association of Hoteliers."

171 The outfit sent by the American Association of Hoteliers to Bing Crosby was undoubtedly a brilliant stroke of genius. From that moment on, jeans were given clearance at functions that were not really casual.

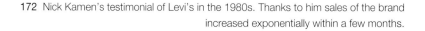

172 Nick Kamen's testimonial of Levi's in the 1980s. Thanks to him sales of the brand increased exponentially within a few months.

173 In the 1990s jeans underwent a genuine revolution thanks to companies in the fashion world that turned them into a sensation and highly desirable item. Stone washing and the contrived worn look were tested out by every fashion label.

On the Waterfront came out only a few years later in 1954, followed by *Rebel Without a Cause*. All the youth of America and beyond lined up next to Marlon Brando and James Dean. Jeans became the symbol of youth, of rebellion, of protest—at times sacrilegious—and culminated in little less than a decade in the counterculture of *Easy Rider* and a Dennis Hopper hippy dressed in denim from head to toe. These were the 1970s, years of civic responsibility and youth culture; dressing was an act of denunciation and every article of clothing came with its own moral, illustrating a particular *Weltanschauung* inspired by flower-power and the demilitarization of the world. The individual was likewise collectivized through the personal act of dressing himself. Perhaps it was precisely for this reason that the runway that arose in the early 1980s seemed—ironically—revolutionary. The first ones were directed at women, as in the campaigns organized by Jesus Jeans, signed by Oliviero Toscani in precisely that place on the rear where jeans invite one to follow, or by Calvin Klein with a very young Brooke Shields. But the true sex revolution came in 1985 with Levi's famous "Launderette" TV commercial, in which Nick Kamen stripped in order to stick his Levi 501s in the washing machine. In Britain the sale of 501s increased by 800% in one week. If the style and fashion establishment still had some qualms about choosing denim as the ultimate icon of our time, its commercial success chased all of them away. Fashion houses not only brought denim to the runway, but even created entire lines dedicated to it, as in the case of Armani with Armani jeans, or Versace with Versace Jeans Couture, or Moschino with

Moschino Jeans. Beyond styles, which change decade after decade, denim rooted itself in everyday existence and became a necessity. In those years companies arose—e.g. John Richmond, Roberto Cavalli, and Diesel—whose success was based entirely on jeans. Great commercial empires, these firms owed their success to the manipulation of denim; Richmond used jeans as a poster, with RICH written on them in big brushstrokes; Diesel adulterated them with a strong "underground" feeling, while Cavalli decorated them in a nearly couture manner. But the quality that ultimately granted denim its iconic status was its resistance to time. Denim by its very nature gradually fades with use and laundering. As Daniel Friedman explains, "Jeans grow old by integrating age into themselves, soaking in the adventure and life of the person who wears them." Every wash is a page turned, time writing its memory on an ever-paler background. The bleaching caused by washing transfers the lived event to the point of saturation. This characteristic is so powerful and so genuine that it is has been achieved through artificial aging to make denim more marketable, reducing the process to a mere aesthetic requirement. But, as the semiologist Ugo Volli maintains, "As authentic or simulated as it may be, there remains the rather bizarre fact of the consumer's 'natural' taste, which in the case of jeans means that the new is worth less than the used, and consumption adds value (aesthetic, emotional, social, even economic) to the object." And as Jean Baudrillard entitled his essay, the world changes, but blue jeans do not.

"I've often wished that it was I who had invented blue jeans: the most spectacular, practical, informal, and relaxed clothing item out there. Jeans have expressive power, sex appeal, simplicity—everything I hope for in my clothing."

(Yves Saint Laurent)

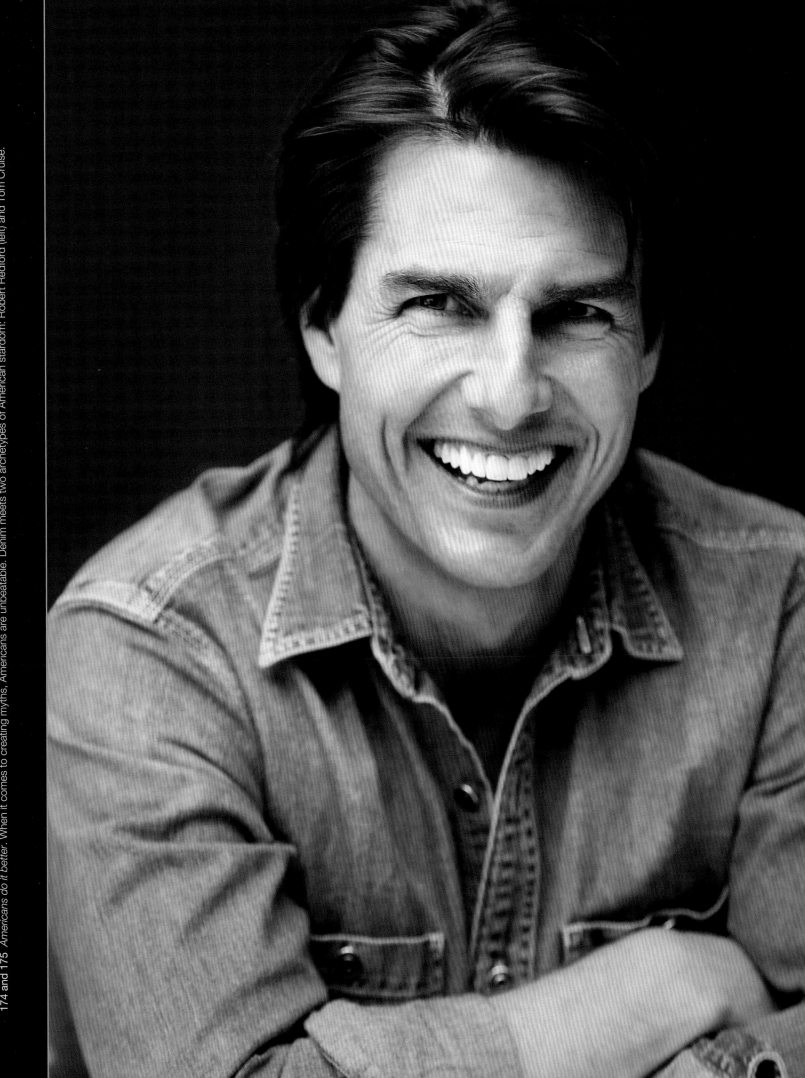

Americans do it better. When it comes to creating myths, Americans are unbeatable. Denim meets two archetypes of American stardom: Robert Redford (left) and Tom Cruise.

MOTORCYCLE JACKET

A QUESTION OF WEATHER

As is the case with all the greatest inventions, it was a single stroke of genius that brought into being one of the most powerful and lasting style icons: the biker jacket. Irving Schott, a son of Russian emigrants who lived and worked in New York City, came up with the historic biker jacket nearly inadvertently, aided by a certain American cultural ingenuity—just as some of his fellow countrymen accidentally invented popcorn or the cheeseburger. In the early 1900s, Irving began working in a textile manufacturing plant, but later, in 1913, he and his brother Jack founded Schott Bros. in a basement on the Lower East Side, and began selling a lined leather raincoat from door to door with some degree of success. This led to their collaboration with the Beck family, the country's largest distributor of Harley-Davidson products. In 1920, Irving Schott began working on new items for the Harley collection and started learning about the biker community. Until that moment the world of motorcycles was the furthest thing from the Schott brothers' mind, especially in the case of Irving, who did not even know how to drive a car. At the same time, however, Irving realized that there was no garment strong and comfortable enough for a biker. Naturally the invention of the zipper (which occurred the year that Schott Bros. was established) greatly facilitated the creation of the ideal garment for the new fashion in motorcycles.

176 The style worn by Marlon Brandon is the Schott Perfecto 613 One Star. The American actor was practically unknown at the time of the *Wild One* as was probably the leather jacket, popular only in the biker community.

178 and 179 The Schott Perfecto 118 is the most famous worldwide. It's made from the "Naked Cowhide" of a young bull with no wax or chemical treatments.

The diagonal zipper was a true stroke of genius: it closed more snugly at the neck, blocked the wind, and above all made it easier to bend forward. In addition, soft leather made the jacket more ergonomic and all movement easier. A "perfecto" garment for every biker—the Spanish nickname for it actually derives from the founder's favorite cigar brand. Initially sales of the studded leather jacket or *chiodo*—as it was translated into Italian—were sluggish because it differed greatly from the long jacket that everyone usually wore in that period. In his simplicity, Irving Schott did something revolutionary—he designed everything with an eye for utility rather than style. That's hard to believe about a garment that later became a fashion icon of the twentieth century. In 1947, a group of bikers in Hollister, California, who called themselves the Boozefighters, sparked a minor rebellion, so much so that a photograph of one of the rebels wearing a leather jacket ended up on the cover of *Life* magazine. It was this news event that inspired László Benedek to shoot his 1953 movie *The Wild One* with Marlon Brando. The image of Marlon/Johnny Strabler, head of the Black Rebel Motorcycle Club wearing a black biker jacket made its way around the world and, aside from canonizing the American actor, bound the studded jacket inextricably to the idea of rebellion, liberty, and strong individualism, which immediately elevated it to Olympian status. As Jason Schott—representing the fourth generation of the family that still runs the business— has remarked, "The bad boy aesthetic acquired by the jacket was absolutely unintentional," adding, "the truth is that my family was always focused on the company and not on its perception by the outside world. That's how Irving set it up." That's not how things turned out, however. From Brando on, things escalated relentlessly, and greasers in the United States as well as rockers in England transformed the studded jacket into a symbol of youthful rebellion, with a look that was rendered equally irreverent through fetishistic and sexual innuendo. 1955 marked the death of James Dean, the "rebel without a cause," whose image in a black leather jacket straddling a motorcycle with a cigarette dangling from his lips contributed not a little to reinforcing the idea of the "Perfecto" as an article of dress for restless and damned souls.

180 The Perfecto is a garment made entirely in the USA. Matching tailoring techniques to the needs of bikers, the Schott family has perfected a highly specialized procedure that has made its products the leaders in the industry.

181 Given the Perfecto's good fortune, Schott & Co. needed a very large venue in which to manufacture and distribute its jackets—so large that it was necessary to move around the shop by electric vehicles, as founder Irving Schott often did.

interesting profile. "Hard-core" seems to be the motto of everyone—musicians or actors—who wear the studded jacket on or off the set. In 1974, the Ramones appeared wearing black studded jackets on the stage of CBGB in New York, making Legs McNeil, founder of *Punk* magazine, observe: "Those guys were so impressive in their studded jackets on stage." The rock-punk aesthetic—all the rage in those years—helped boost the "ugly and bad" reputation that the studded biker's jacket maintains to this day. As in the case of Sid Vicious of the Sex Pistols, who was captured in his leather jacket in 1978 when arrested on charges of the murder of his girlfriend Nancy Spungen. Sid's story made such a huge impression that it was revived in the 1986 movie, *Sid & Nancy*, starring Gary Oldman and Chloe Webb. In the early 1980s, another American idol, Bruce Springsteen, confirmed his identity as an angry individual by dressing in jeans, a T-shirt, and a leather jacket; Michael Jackson became the most famous singer in music history by wearing a red and black leather jacket, while playing the role of an evil werewolf in the music video *Thriller*. One star beyond the film and music industry is worth mentioning as he contributed so much to the tough look: Fonzie of *Happy Days*, who entertained us for nearly two decades with his portrayal of 1960s American youth. The same could be said for John Travolta in *Grease*, the epitome of all greasers, and one who enlivened their reputation. By this time we're in 1978; a mere year later Mel Gibson played an angry and vindictive cop in *Mad Max*; the character's black filthy jacket well captured his restlessness and rage. But it was Arnold Schwarzenegger's 1984 *Terminator* that was to pull the studded jacket into the future. Nor can we forget about Johnny Depp in one of his early performances as the bad guy—though in this case with a kind heart—in *Cry Baby* of 1990. The biker's jacket instantly defines its wearer, immediately embodies the personality and lifestyle of the person who dons it. As Jason Schott notes, "When you look at a leather jacket you can almost feel the emotion of the person wearing it." Genuine connoisseurs of the genre use it as an open coffer on which to attach, staple, and stick objects and things of no stylistic value that serve as statements of cultural belonging or as mere mementos. Along with members of the movie and music industry, the motorcycling community has continued to nurture the myth of the "Perfecto" as an item expressing their personality that improves over time.

182 The motorcycle jacket is closely bound to the underground culture of rock and punk. The Ramones were one its most vital and important proponents. Back then it was impossible to be transgressive without wearing a leather jacket, symbol of the utter rejection of bourgeois values.

Many bikers wear old jackets that they have been mending for over thirty years, but often leave parts of them damaged as testimony of their experiences. The leather jacket has therefore covered an infinite variety of masculine sectors and types: from Tom Cruise in *Top Gun* to Michael Paré in *Eddie and the Cruiser* and Keanu Reeves and Laurence Fishburne in *The Matrix*, from Gary Cooper in *For Whom the Bell Tolls* to Brad Pitt in *The Fight Club*. However, the biker's jacket has also been able to conquer the glossy world of fashion, both on and off the catwalk. Yves Saint Laurent introduced it in the 1960 Dior collection, and Hedi Slimane, his current successor in the new Saint Laurent brand, has not only "adopted it as her uniform, but has also endowed it with new glamour…" In the golden years of fashion it was reinterpreted by Jean-Paul Gaultier, Montana, Gianni Versace, and above all Comme des Garçons. In fact today anyone can gain access to a bit of the myth through its many designer versions. There is not a single actor of the new generation—from Ryan Gosling to Justin Timberlake—who has not worn one in his personal or public life. Were we to ask Marlon Brando today the question that made him famous in *The Wild One*, "But Johnny, what are you rebelling against?" he would probably offer the same reply: "What would you suggest?"

184 Hollywood stars contribute to the diffusion of great American myths such as the Perfecto. In the futuristic road movie *Mad Max* Mel Gibson flaunted the leather jacket in an unreal dimension, utterly different from the one hitherto seen on the big screen.

185 A very young Brad Pitt immortalized in an "American Graffiti" style biker jacket and boots, which he retained in another movie that made history, *Fight Club*.

BOOTS

FROM THE KNEE DOWN

In 1977, Billy Joel sang about "engineer boots" in his *Scenes from an Italian Restaurant*. The boots in question were the ones made famous in the 1950s by Marlon Brando and James Dean, and that after nearly half a century of trial and tribulation—and nearly a century since their conception—had become the boots par excellence all over the world. One of America's earliest shoe companies, which, together with Red Wing Shoes and Frye, pioneered the boot industry, was founded in Chippewa Falls, Wisconsin in 1901. By 1937, Chippewa, already supplying half the United States work boots, began realizing that industry and agriculture were growing and changing, especially when it came to management, and that their personnel traveling for business had to look a bit less boorish than they had hitherto been allowed. Though placing faith in their own status, engineers and inspectors of yards were looking for boots that were more linear and simple. Some modifications were introduced, starting with the riding boot: its contour was simplified, its height raised to 43 cm (17 inches), its laces replaced by a side buckle, the quality of its leather improved, and its manufacturing process replaced with the more distinguished Goodyear system, used in the production of elegant English shoes.

186 Like five-pocket jeans, biker boots represent the quintessence of the American pop culture. Cowboys, bikers, and blue-collar workers are all categories embodying the primordial values of this country.

During the Depression, Chippewa is credited for inventing Engineer-style boots.

Thus was born the Engineer boot, now more commonly known as the biker boot. The current definition obviously takes into account the accessory's success in the everyday life of Americans. The West Coast Shoe Company released its own version in 1939, and in 1941 Red Wing Shoes, inspired by railroad engineers, did the same but added a piece of stretch fabric to the outer side of the boot in order to facilitate movement. Seeing the quality and toughness of these boots, the budding biker community immediately took an interest in the accessory. These new boots could be abused and splattered with oil without risk of wear and tear; they also offered the legs greater protection from sparks, and, lacking laces, reduced the danger of snags. Researching the biker's needs in depth, Chippewa created a new model that was better suited to the dynamics of the motorcyclist's life. It lowered the height of the boots to 28 cm (11 ft), making it easier to switch gears, and enlarged the heel to improve its grip on the pedal. Thus emerged the final model, which motorcyclists instantly declared as their one and only type of footwear from now 'til forever, inadvertently turning it into a symbol of rebellion and transgression. Marlon Brando in *The Wild One*, the trouble-maker James Dean in *Rebel Without a Cause*, then the fugitive Steve McQueen in *The Great Escape*, and the subversive Peter Fonda in *Easy Rider* of 1969—all crystallized the image of the leather-jacket, motorcycle-boot clad rebel.

188 hippewa resisted and continued manufacturing through a historical period as grave as the Great Depression of the 1930s.

The Wild One, a 1953 outlaw biker film, starring American film icon, Marlon Brando

189 top In the movie *The Wild One*, Marlon Brando became the symbol of the American bikers of the 1950s. His boots were manufactured by Chippewa.

189 bottom Chippewa boots are one of the linchpins of American pragmatism. Comfortable, durable, and simple in design, they are made to last, and have done so for more than a century.

For devotees, this form of footwear has gone beyond being a mere accessory to becoming a symbol that represents an attitude towards life and a truly American style. Upon returning from the war, many veterans became motorcyclists as if to challenge 1950s bourgeois respectability. The basic items of their apparel became symbols of a choice—that of simple but well-ingrained values, of a culture that did not change.

After *Easy Rider*, most movies about bikers became odes to freedom packed with heroic romanticism—a choice of lifestyle that set indomitable individuality above rules. Willem Dafoe played one of those motorcyclists rampant in South America in the 1982 film, *The Loveless*, directed by Kathryn Bigelow; Matt Dillon and Tom Cruise played young drifters in Francis Ford Coppola's masterpiece, *The Outsiders* (1983). Boots came to resemble travel companions, and, paraphrasing a well-known song, served as witnesses of their owners' adventures. In *Fandango* (1985) Kevin Costner's boots recount a coming-of-age story. We encounter the same solitary traveling soul in *Out of Africa*'s Robert Redford (1985), who added a new detail to the iconic image of the boot.

190 Through their monolithic appearance, biker boots represent an attitude to life. Transcending fashion and fads, they have always remained simply themselves.

191 John Wayne posing with his son and a pair of boots that the actor used in nearly all his movies.

The sense of belonging triggered by the biker boot is clear in the 1991 movie *Harley Davidson and the Marlboro Man*, in which Don Johnson and Mickey Rourke represent two different Americas through their boots—that of the biker and that of the cowboy.

Meanwhile in Europe, the subcultures related to music and art appropriated boots exactly as they did the Perfecto, leaning towards the provocative, fetishistic aspect of leather. British actor Peter Cook in a flawless, all-black uniform in the early 1970s is a genuine representative of this trend, as are various punk-rock bands like the Clash, which alternated between biker and combat boots. An element with so many connotations can hardly avoid cutting across boundaries; these boots have done just fine after crossing the ocean, migrating from bikers to music while maintaining their revolutionary allure intact.

The flexibility of the accessory is also what impacted fashion, which quickly appropriated the item and recast it in various ways in the collections of ever designer—so much so that the boot became the personal uniform among some of them, is in the case of John Galliano and Karl Lagerfeld. Their landing in the fashion system completes the cycle and definitively blesses them with eternal, unlimited success.

192 In old factories in Wisconsin or Massachusetts, such as Frye, boots are manufactured in a nearly sacred atmosphere inside huge cathedral-like factories—today veritable monuments of the American history.

192-193 It was 1863 when John A. Frye sold his first pair of boots in his store on Elm Street in Marlboro, Massachusetts. That first pair is now housed in the Marlboro Historical Society along with other Frye memorabilia, and is regarded as a national symbol. In 1890, Frye became the country's largest manufacturer.

T-SHIRT

SEDUCTIVE BASICS

"I guess I strike you as the unrefined type." It was with this wisecrack while taking off his sweaty T-shirt in a scene with Vivien Leigh that the young Marlon Brando made his debut on the big screen. The fame of the T-shirt arose precisely from *A Streetcar Named Desire*, a major Hollywood production in 1951. The birth of a star such as Brando also marked the popular success of a garment that until then had been considered a purely practical item in a man's wardrobe. The seductive and voluptuous chest of the young actor shook the culture of the 1950s, still steeped in bourgeois respectability. If to this we add that it was only four years later that James Dean, another rising star of American cinema, wore one in the tormented role of Jim Stark, the rebellious teenager in *Rebel Without a Cause*, we come to understand how a simple cotton undershirt became an icon, a symbol of freedom and youthful defiance. Even more than a symbol, however, the T-shirt almost immediately became a medium, an emanation of the person who wore it, a poster for any battle. A T-shirt is a blank sheet on which any message can be written. So great is the garment's historical and social success that it mirrors the century's history in a nutshell.

195 The white T-shirt is archetypical of male sensuality. Marlon Brando was the perfect embodiment of this ideal, innate beauty that until that point men had not manifested even in movies.

If we are to imagine a hypothetical gallery of T-shirt worn by celebrities and especially regular people (who have used them to champion political causes or to display trendy slogans), we can begin by looking at the first model created for the U.S. Navy in 1913. During World War I, however, the Marines realized that the inhabitants of southern Europe wore a more lightweight and comfortable version in cotton. They instantly adopted it, and upon returning to their homeland, spread it throughout the country. By this point, an everyday item for all Americans—and not only for them—its real lucky break occurred in 1942 after a photo of a soldier in a military T-shirt appeared on the cover of *Life* magazine. Actually, signs of the garment's expressive potential date even earlier than the movie icons mentioned above. In 1948, Thomas E. Dewey, the governor of New York, used one to promote his candidacy for the White House by printing on it the words "Dew it for Dewey." In 1952, Dwight D. Eisenhower did the same with better luck using the phrase: "I like Ike." Since then, the course of the T-shirt has been all downhill and interspersed with icons that signify a cultural revolution, in the same way that it itself was the forerunner of the *brevitas* that technology, cell phones, and social networks have brought to the twenty-first century. The 1960s appropriated it as their own, treating it as a staple of juvenile fashion and the rock generation.

196 Practicality, comfort, and low cost: these are the ingredients of the T-shirt's success in the armed forces of the U.S. Army. Despite its simplicity, it became an integral part of the Marines' uniform and from there soon spread to the general public.

197 At the outbreak of World War II, the U.S. army appeared in a T-shirt both in its home country and abroad. A statement that did not go unobserved.

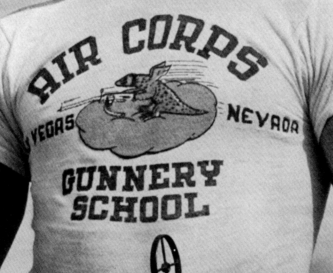

LIFE

AIR CORPS

VEGAS   NEVADA

GUNNERY
SCHOOL

JULY 13, 1942 **10** CENTS
YEARLY SUBSCRIPTION $4.50

198 Richard Gere in the movie *Bloodbrothers* played the role of a construction worker.

199 In love with all types of races and the thrill of speed, Steve McQueen was perhaps the perfect endorsement of the T-shirt, which speaks of strong passion, motorcycles, and utter independence and freedom from strategy and obligations, as was the case with his career.

New printing techniques turned it into a medium of wearable art—for conveying messages and protests, but also advertising products. Two U.S. companies took the first steps towards using the T-shirt for this new end. One was Monster, a California firm that began manufacturing T-shirts with symbols and motifs associated with the Grateful Dead and the ever-increasing use of marijuana, and that later became particularly famous for its print of Che Guevara's face. The other was Warren Dayton, a pioneering artist in various printing techniques who used political cartoons and cultural icons of various kinds. He was the first to turn the face of César Chávez into a symbol of social opposition at a time when Chávez was still a young activist. Protest in those years— especially in the early 1970s—was not only directed at politics but also at conventions and social life. In the golden age of rock and roll, songs spoke of the desecration of customs, the protest against the family as institution, and sexual conventions. It was this reason that led to the resounding fame of the image (a mouth with a tongue sticking out provocatively) on the Rolling Stones T-shirt. Soon afterwards, Madonna wore the "Italians do it better" T-shirt, which alluded to sex in a double sense but with a new and updated explosive power by being declared by a woman. Yet it was precisely the transition from the 1970s to the 1980s that secured the T-shirt a dominant role in pop culture by superimposing marketing onto its social and demonstrative function. By then every company, every society, but also every single person was assigning the T-shirt the function of communicating personal or business messages, and disseminating logos or marketing strategies. The success of Milton Glaser's phrase "I love NY" (*love* spelled with a heart) and dedicated to New York is a prime example of this phenomenon.

200 Marketing has taken a definitive hold of the T-shirt. Not only items, but even cities and towns can be advertised on a white cotton shirt.

201 top A T-shirt is for everyone; these days newsstands and stores worldwide display dozens of T-shirts with all types of images. Among the most popular are political symbols from Che Guevara to Mao.

201 bottom Irreverently sticking out its tongue, the red mouth printed on shirts and objects of all kind presents us with the hedonism of the Rolling Stones while implying the dictum: "It's only rock 'n' roll, but we like it."

The new casual wear modeled on Don Johnson of *Miami Vice* included a T-shirt with the Armani logo beneath every kind of outfit; thus fashion began to use the garment as a cheap way to advertise particular brands. T-shirts played a significant role in the late 1980s thanks to the mania for logos. From Calvin Klein to Armani, from Gap to FUBU, from Ralph Lauren to American Apparel all the way down to Chanel's famous double C, there was not a house that did not use the T-shirt to create a "niche" for itself, and at the same time to surgically implant brand awareness. The London underground designer, Katharine Hamnett's use of a giant caption on an oversized T-shirt in the early 1980s seemed an isolated phenomenon; but this style in fact became so famous that it was later adopted by all luxury establishments. With its enormous media power, fashion permanently sealed the T-shirt's fate as a means of mass communication. In recent decades, excessive exhibitionism has turned amusing and ironic self-referential comments into the last frontier of T-shirt messages, from ironic phrases such as "My parents went to Las Vegas and all I got was this lousy T-shirt," to groupie fashion statements such as "I'll tell you who's the boss, Kate Moss," which brought success to the new British brand, House of Holland. To be cutting, impertinent, perhaps offensive has thus become the final frontier of this garment, through which stars sometimes engage in dialogue or offend each other from afar. The world of celebrities provides an endless source of subject matter for this article of dress: one of its most popular current manufacturers is, in fact, called Stylestalker. Thus from groupies to stalkers, the T-shirt once again is a symbol of the times.

202 As a teenager, Henry Holland fooled around with the T-shirt. The irony and sympathetic irreverence of his T-shirts have been popular since the launch of the House of Holland label in 2008.

203 Giorgio Armani, in his apartment in Milan, wearing a dark-blue T-shirt, symbol of his style.

BOMBER JACKET

FROM THE MILITARY TO COUNTER-CULTURE

In a recent interview, former DJ and London night scene figure Chris Sullivan spoke about his cult clothing item, namely, the bomber jacket, whose widespread success he attributed to its extreme functionality; it is a garment that transcends fashion—so much so that in certain ways it has become a classic. Qualities associated with the military, such as portability, simplicity, and aesthetics, have often been seen to lead to the success of a menswear item. The bomber jacket is no exception; indeed it reinforces this axiom by demonstrating, throughout the century of its existence, its capability to speak to different generations and cultures which are poles apart. Its success among the mods, and later the skinheads and punks in England, can be misleading. The origins of the bomber jacket are not in fact Anglo-Saxon, but American. Two Hollywood myths, utterly different in terms of history and character but much alike in their celebration of restlessness and rebellion, endowed the garment with a deeply masculine quality, bordering on *machismo*, that definitely shaped its future success. James Dean in *Rebel Without a Cause* and Steve McQueen in *The Great Escape* helped define the concept of a distinctly American "casual style" by combining several items from the male wardrobe with lots of personality. The bomber jacket enjoyed such widespread popularity that by 1965 it was being worn by Alain Delon in Europe, precisely because of his predilection for playing the lovable rogue.

204 Maverick, or non-conformist, or the unleashed dog is Tom Cruise's nickname in the movie *Top Gun*. It's no coincidence that in many scenes he wears a bomber, itself a symbol of dissidence and rebellion against any rules.

This was the version that determined its course in contemporary fashion, except within the bracket of British subcultures, where its meaning was grossly distorted, especially in the excesses associated with skinheads. It was Steve McQueen who wore it once again in 1980, in his final movie, *The Hunter*. Two films associated with the origins of the flight jacket were important to its success; first, *The Right Stuff* with Sam Shepard in 1983; and second, *Top Gun* with Tom Cruise in 1986, which, not incidentally, raised him to the status of matinee idol thanks to a blend of testosterone, coolness, and romanticism. The first bomber jacket was produced by the American Air Force in 1917. Over the course of years and several wars, various models followed, each marked by seals similar to those displayed on airplanes, but basically divisible into two broad categories: leather and nylon. The two iconic fur-lined leather jackets were known as A-2 and G-1, while the MA-1 was the green nylon model with orange lining, whose lighter version was the L-2B.

206 In the recent history of the United States few people can claim to have influenced the attire of their country as profoundly as did James Dean. Dead by age 24, he was the symbol of the cultural revolution of the 1950s.

207 Steve McQueen wore the bomber in numerous movies, including *The Great Escape* and *The Hunter*, his last film, shot in 1980.

Born from the need to protect pilots, who at the time were flying open-frame, single-seat aircraft, the aforementioned styles stopped being manufactured after several years (ca 1942, in the case of the first two), but were so successful that the MA-1 in particular was marketed—and initially possibly even smuggled—throughout Europe (to European armies and private aficionados) after 1949 by Alpha Industries. Various revisions and upgrades continued to be introduced until the 1990s, when the MA-1 came to be used by ground crews only. The modifications affected chiefly the finish and materials, which were improved on the basis of new inventions and technologies, while the number of color combinations—such an important factor in the bomber's success, especially in the case of the orange-lined army green jacket—was reduced. The first model came in blue with a green lining, but was soon changed to green and orange. It was joined by a version in camouflage, which was used during the Vietnam War. In the constant interplay between military and civilian attire, so characteristic of the twentieth century, the bomber was a symptomatic case of value inversion and the alteration of original meaning. As *New York Times* journalist Holly Brubach wrote in 1997, "The imitation of the military uniform has triumphed over the original prototype." This claim applied mostly to the U.S., where military heroes and Hollywood stars engaged in a unique cultural exchange.

208 Marilyn Monroe wearing an MA-1 with a fur collar during her visit to Korea.

209 top The Tuskegee Army Flying School was the first academy to train American pilots of color, and class SE 43 K was the first to wear the A-1 at this key moment in U.S. aviation history.

209 bottom The Bomber A-2 Deco in leather: the model of American pilots par excellence. The embroidered patch shows a Thunderbird flying in a red sun, while the treatment of the goatskin makes this jacket suitable for temperatures as low as 32 °F.

210 Juvenile restlessness goes well with the proletarian and revolutionary symbolism of the bomber. In Britain skinheads are the lunatic fringe of a society that suffered a sharp economic and social crisis in the 1980s.

211 Like all Alpha Industries bomber jackets, the L-2B model required that inside it be printed a message in various languages that made it possible to identify the soldier who wore it

In Europe and especially in England, on the other hand, the anti-establishment movements of the 1970s and 1980s led mods, punks, and skinheads to adopt the bomber as a uniform and symbol of protest that soon expanded into positions that were sometimes difficult to embrace. The fashion of this urban culture arose from the values and taste of the early skinheads—from the rude boy to the mod—but was likewise an expression of the working class to which they belonged as well as of the social confrontations between them and authorities and people of higher standing. The reasons behind this choice of garment were sought in the lifestyle of the early skinheads and their desire to rebel against the dominant culture. What they needed above all were rugged, clean garments that were easy to spot in a crowd, suitable for manual labor, and conforming to the image of the underclass. In this sense, the distinction between the leather and nylon models assumed interesting cultural and social significance. For the mods, as Chris Sullivan himself recounts, the leather bomber was a sort of evolved form of the jacket that they had worn in college. Subsequently, its high price made it more fashionable and enabled its diffusion in an alternative but chic environment (the music and theater world), while the cheaper, nylon version became popular among skinheads. The phenomenon quickly turned global as recounted in *American History X*, the movie that made Edward Norton famous. Despite its nationalistic origins, the bomber has retained its sense of protest, which has been tapped into and conveyed by rap music. It was for this reason that not only the punk rock bands of the 1970s and 1980s, but also American rappers yielded to the seduction of the garment, and Onyx and Naughty by Nature chose it as their *urbanwear* uniform in the 1990s. Kanye West further enhanced its popularity in 2013 by integrating it as a gadget in his Yeezus Tour (he wore it while performing *Black Skinhead*). Thoroughly appropriated by fashion, the bomber jacket has been reinterpreted in thousands of fabrics and combinations. Like no other article of dress, the MA-1 echoes the prophetic words of Diana Vreeland, who, in a bygone era of innocence, proclaimed that military uniforms would become the casualwear of the twentieth century.

SNEAKERS

WINGED FEET

Sneakers are not only shoes. They're a cult. From the beginning, the world of sneakers and that of sports have been inextricably bound, generating—especially since the 1990s—genuine fanaticism. Nothing recounts their history better than the classification of their most important styles. Cult followers of the genre exist with the purpose of snatching up the latest model as soon as it appears on the market. Fanaticism goes hand in hand with collecting, and legends about impassioned youth—called "sneaker heads"—prepared to do anything to secure a piece of the myth run rampant. In the United States they have grown from being mere fans to true professionals trading in one-of-a-kind items. At times, however, even thousands of dollars will not succeed in making collectors yield—as in the case of the 18-year-old Jonathon Rodriguez, who would not surrender his Nike Yuzzy 2 Reds autographed by Kanye West for the hefty sum of $98,000. But the sneaker cannot be dismissed as a purely "adolescent thing." Actually, it is definitely the most cross-the-board item in the memory of contemporary fashion. From the 35 million pairs manufactured in 1940 the number has risen to 135 million twenty years later, and so on exponentially to the present.

213 The Yezzy 2 Reds autographed by Kanye West that belong to the American Jonathan Rodriguez, who would not give them up despite an offer of $98,000.

213

Such is the distance travelled by the first sneaker, created in 1923 when the famous U.S. basketball player, Chuck Taylor, put on a shoe designed and produced by Marquis Converse for basketball. It was thus in honor of the champion that the iconic Chuck Taylor All-Stars, the best-selling shoe of all time, was created. A mere year later the brothers Adolf and Rudolf Dassler founded the Dassler brand, which exploded after Jesse Owens won four Olympic gold medals in Berlin while wearing their shoe. Afterwards, the two brothers separated, and Adolf Dassler established Adidas in 1948, while his brother Rudolf founded Puma.

214 The actor-singer Rick Springfield during a break in a concert in California in 1974.

214-215 The classic model of Converse All Star had to cover the ankle. Indeed when the version "cut" below the ankle entered the market in 1957, it did not enjoy a similar success either in the playing field, or with the public.

Ten years later, in 1958, Joe and Jeff Foster, firmly following the family tradition (their father, Joseph, had invented the first spiked running shoes), set up their company, Reebok, a name derived from an inflection of *rhebok*, the fastest-running gazelle in Africa. Ten years later, in 1967, Phil Knight, a young economics professor, and Bill Bowerman, his coach at the University of Oregon, created Nike. But it was only in 1971 with the help of a graphic designer student, Carolyn Davidson, that the Swoosh—the symbol in the logo recalling *The Winged Nike* of Samothrace—came into being. Thus by the early 1970s, the leading figures in the most important clothing revolution of the twentieth century were already on track. And so it was to be. The giants of the sport shoe soon figured out that music and sport were and would be the key to world success. A heteronym created from the term "Adidas" captures the meaning of this deep bond: "All Day I Dream About Sports." It was also precisely in the 1970s that hip hop and rap spread from the suburbs of American cities to the rest of the world, opening the road to Contemporary R&B. When Run DMC appeared completely in Adidas from head to toe in the early 1980s, the sport brand's sphere of influence spread to everyday life. Sneakers became a lifestyle. The die had been cast; street style imposed itself on and changed the rules of the world.

216 Adolf Dassler, the founder of Adidas, in the company of the same name in 1948, when he was still working with his brother Rudolf.

217 *My Adidas* was the song sung by Run DMC in 1986. During a concert at Madison Square Garden, in which the band asked fans to raise their Adidas during the song, the German giant enlisted the group as an international endorser.

In those same years, a minor revolution occurred on basketball courts when Nike first named a model after a player. Michael Jordan played a game in Air Jordans 1, which went down in history as "banned" because David Stern, Commissioner of the NBA, banned them for their color.

218 Michael Jordan has often been called one of the best athletes of the last century. Nike Air Jordans derived their name from his nickname, which he earned for his ability and his spectacular maneuvers.

219 Jordan was reprimanded during a game for wearing Air Jordans, thus promoting their launch. The motive may seem absurd but regulations forbade it—a rule that nevertheless was advantageous to Nikes and increased their sales.

Reebok, in turn, created the Pump and introduced technology into the world of sneakers. Its patent was based on the concept of the "personalized fit", as the shoe was designed in such a way as to adjust perfectly to any foot. Reebok began important collaborations with musicians of the caliber of 50 Cent and Swizz Beatz and athletes such as Allen Iverson, who were fascinated by this innovation. But the high point came with Shaquille O'Neal, the famous basketball player as well as rapper and actor, to whom Reebok dedicated the model known as Shaq Attaq. For this reason he became so symbolic a figure in "sneaker culture" as to declare: "I only want to play basketball, drink Pepsi, and wear Reebok." This seems to echo the philosophy voiced by LL Cool J in 1986 in the *Football Rap* soundtrack for the movie *Wildcats*. From that point on, there have been endless collaborations between sneaker brands and celebrities, the most recent being those between Adidas and both Kanye West and Pharrell Williams. A similar strategy has been followed by fashion brands, among which the most success collaborations have definitely been those between the designer Jeremy Scott and once again Adidas, or between Riccardo Tisci at Givenchy and Nike. The new millennium has decreed that sneakers have not only conquered fashion but are also the new object of desire. But who are the true leading figures of this passion? Let us recall the key moments of their success from past to present.

220 The Reebok Pump was the first shoe in which the technology of the "Pump" system could be activated for a custom fit.

221 top A pair of original Adidas conceived by fashion designer Jeremy Scott in 2012.

221 bottom The Nike designed by Riccardo Tisci for Givenchy established the new alliance between internationally renowned designers and sneakers.

221

AUTHOR

GIUSEPPE CECCARELLI is a journalist specializing in fashion and costume. His professional experience spans both print and web, and includes television. He began his career working on sites such as modaonline.it and CNN Style. He then entered fashion publishing, first in the Class Editori group, then for seven years at *L'Uomo Vogue*. In 2011 he began freelancing and now handles photography, texts, and interviews for the monthly magazine *Gentlemen*, affiliated with *Milano Finanza*. Over the years he has also served as casting director at runway shows in Paris and Milan and participated in international talent competitions. Currently he is collaborating with other men's magazines around the world and working as an image and style consultant for a number of companies.

NY Daily News Archive/Getty Images: page 59

Marc Oeder/Getty Images: page 5

Omikron Omikron/Getty Images: page 110

Francois Pages/Paris Match/Getty Images: page 141

Paramount Pictures/Archive Photos/Getty Images: page 204

Jay Paull/Getty Images: page 30

Jean-Marie Périer/Photo12: page 109

PhotoQuest/Getty Images: page 208

Photos 12/Alamy Stock Photo: page 174

Pictorial Parade/Archive Photos/Getty Images: page 99

picture alliance/Fryderyk Gabowicz: page 172

© Picture Alliance/Photoshot: page 199

Alessia Pierdomenico/Bloomberg/Getty Images: page 162

Popperfoto/Getty Images: page 83

Andreas Rentz/Getty Images: page 125 top

© Retna Pictures/Photoshot: page 175

© Mark Richardson/Alamy Stock Photo/IPA: page 167

Jack Robinson/Hulton Archive/Getty Images: page 28

Rue Des Archives/AGF: pages 66, 153 top, 184, 206, 207

© Rue des Archives/DILTZ/Bridgeman Images: page 100

Andreas Schlegel/Getty Images: page 186

Richard Sears provided by Mikki Ansin/Liaison Agency/Getty Images: page 147

Silver Screen Collection/Getty Images: page 132

Oleksandr Sobko/Alamy/IPA: pages 8-9

Chip Somodevilla/Getty Images: page 51 bottom

Edward Steichen/Condé Nast/Getty Images: page 102 right

Gus Stewart/Redferns/Getty Images: page 182

Rob Stothard/Getty Images: page 31

Victor VIRGILE/GAMMA-RAPHO: page 134

Wavebreak/iStockphoto: pages 46-47

David Willis/NBCU Photo Bank/Getty Images: page 48

Kevin Winter/Getty Images: page 125 bottom

ullstein bild/ullstein bild/Getty Images: pages 168-169, 170, 216

Universal/Getty Images: page 155

Universal Images Group/Getty Images: page 201

© UPPA/Photoshot: page 50 top

CHRIS YOUNG/AFP/Getty Images: page 16

Courtesy of:

Acquascutum London: pages 102 left, 103

Albertelli: pages 24, 25

Alfa Industries: pages 209 bottom, 211

Alice Made This: page 53 top left

Asprey London: page 52 bottom left

Cesare Attolini: page 18

Bruno Aveillan (Santoni): page 94 top

Bell & Ross: page 65

Borsalino: pages 112 bottom, 114, 115

Breitling: pages 61 top, 64 top

Brooks Brothers Button Down and Brooks Brothers Regimental: page 33

Bulgari: page 53 top center

Camiceria Ambrosiana: page 32

Loretta Caponi: page 136

Cartier: pages 53 bottom, 55, 56

Chippewa: pages 188, 189

Deakin & Francis: page 52 top

Dege & Skinner: pages 126, 127

Derek Rose: page 135 top

Diesel: page 173

E. Marinella Napoli: pages 44, 45

Edward Green: page 87

Fred Perry: page 143

Frye Company: pages 190, 192, 193

Hanro: page 135 bottom left

Henry Poole & Co Ltd.: page 15

House of Holland: page 202

Giovanni Inglese: page 27

IWC: pages 57, 64 bottom

Lacoste: pages 139,140

Les Ateliers Louis Moinet: page 69

Levi's: page 171

Longines: pages 58-59, 59 bottom, 60

Luxottica: pages 150, 152 bottom, 153 bottom, 156,157

Olivia Magris: page 116

Marini 1899 Srl: pages 84, 85

Moreschi: pages 96, 97

Franck Muller: page 68

Museo Salvatore Ferragamo, Firenze: pages 92, 93

Mark Peckmezian (Hermès): pages 42,43

Nike: pages 219, 221

Jacobs & Co: page 49 top

Olatz: page 135 bottom right

Omega: pages 61 bottom, 67 bottom right

Patek Philippe: page 71

Susanna Pozzoli (Santoni): page 95

Press Office Church's: pages 81, 88-89 bottom

Press Office Church's/Paolo Barbi: 90, 91

Press Office Car Shoe: pages 159, 160, 160-161

Press Office Panizza: page 117

Rolex: pages 62, 63, 67 top right

Rubinacci Spa: page 53 top right

Paolo Scafore: page 94 bottom

Schott NYC: pages 179, 180, 181

Christopher Simon Sykes (Anderson & Sheppard): pages 12, 13

Stetson: page 111

Tag Heuer: page 66 bottom

Tod's Group: pages 164, 164-165, 165

Trianon: page 52 bottom right

Tricker's: page 86

Turnbull & Asser: pages 2-3

Zimmerli of Switzerland: page 137

Cover

Fabrics are the soul of every custom-tailored men's suit: the choice should be based on the type of garment desired.
© Marc Oeder/Getty Images

Backcover

An advertising campaign by Church's, representing a classic in the British tradition of high-fashion footwear.
© Courtesy of Press Office Church's

The Author would like to thank:
Gerardo Mandara for his expertise and professional assistance,
as well as Andrea Polonio and Barbara Papalini for their support.

The Publisher would like to thank:
Aquascutum London, Alessandra Migliavacca (Parini Associati Srl), Alessandro Agostini (Camiceria
Ambrosiana), Alice Made This, Alice Rosselli (Cartier), Ambra Russo (Maximilian Linz), Anderson
& Sheppard, Andrea Marini (Rolex), Anjeza Sengla (Rubinacci), Angelo Inglese (Giovanni Inglese),
Asprey London, Baumann Sonja (Zimmerli), Bell & Ross, Bulgari, Breitling, Cass Stainton (Dege
& Skinner), Cesare Attolini, Chippewa, Daniele Marini, Daria Missori (Avanguardia srl), Deakin &
Francis, Derek Rose, Euan Denholm (Edward Green), Flavio Cerbone (Church's and Car Shoe Press
Offices), Federica Croci (Tod's Group), Francesca Mirra (IWC), Francesca Piani (Foto Locchi), Ginevra
Montezemolo (Urrà S.A.S. Press Office), Giuseppe Palmieri (Paolo Scafora), Henry Poole & Co, House
of Holland, Jacobs & Co, Jennifer Goldszer (Schott NYC), Laura Bondi (Frank Muller), Laura Salvetti
(Santoni), Les Ateliers Louis Moinet SA, Longines, Lorenzo Lodigiani (Borsalino), Loretta Caponi,
Luigi Bottani (Diesel), Maria Manzitti (Hermès), Matteo Convenevole (Omega), Maurizio Marinella,
Moreschi, Nina Rehmann (Hanro), Olatz, Paola Varani (hub srl), Paolo de Vivo, Piero Albertelli,
Stefania Belloli (Patek Philippe), Tania Shaw (Tricker's), Trianon, Turnbull & Asser, Valentina Castellani
(Grazia Lotti), Yvonne Yuen (Alpha Industries)

WHITE STAR PUBLISHERS

WS White Star Publishers® is a registered trademark
property of White Star s.r.l.

© 2016 White Star s.r.l.
Piazzale Luigi Cadorna, 6
20123 Milan, Italy
www.whitestar.it

Translation: Irina Oryshkevich

ISBN 978-88-544-1060-2
1 2 3 4 5 6   20 19 18 17 16

Printed in China